Apollo 1 and the Space Shuttle *Challenger*: The History of NASA's Two Most Notorious Disasters

By Charles River Editors

Gus Grissom, Ed White, and Roger Chaffee in front of the launch pad 10 days before the disaster

About Charles River Editors

Charles River Editors provides superior editing and original writing services in the digital publishing industry, with the expertise to create digital content for publishers across a vast range of subject matter. In addition to providing original digital content for third party publishers, we also republish civilization's greatest literary works, bringing them to new generations of readers via ebooks.

Introduction

Apollo 1 (January 27, 1967)

The insignia for the Apollo 1 mission

"There's always a possibility that you can have a catastrophic failure, of course; this can happen on any flight; it can happen on the last one as well as the first one. So, you just plan as best you can to take care of all these eventualities, and you get a well-trained crew and you go fly." - Gus Grissom, December 1966

The Apollo space program is the most famous and celebrated in American history, but the first successful landing of men on the Moon during Apollo 11 had complicated roots dating back over a decade, and it also involved one of NASA's most infamous tragedies. Landing on the Moon presented an ideal goal all on its own, but the government's urgency in designing the Apollo program was actually brought about by the Soviet Union, which spent much of the 1950s leaving the United States in its dust (and rocket fuel). In 1957, at a time when people were concerned about communism and nuclear war, many Americans were dismayed by news that the Soviet Union was successfully launching satellites into orbit.

Among those concerned was President Dwight D. Eisenhower, whose space program was clearly lagging a few years behind the Soviets' space program. From 1959-1963, the United States worked toward putting satellites and humans into orbit via the Mercury program, but Eisenhower's administration was already designing plans for the Apollo program by 1960, a year before the first Russian orbited the Earth and two years before John Glenn became the first American to orbit the Earth.

On May 25, 1961, President John F. Kennedy addressed Congress and asked the nation to "commit itself to achieving the goal, before this decade is out, of landing a man on the Moon and returning him safely to the Earth." Given America's inability to even put a man in orbit yet, this seemed like an overly ambitious goal, and it isn't even clear that Kennedy himself believed it possible; after all, he was reluctant to meet NASA Administrator James E. Webb's initial funding requests.

As Apollo 11's name suggests, there were actually a number of Apollo missions that came before, many of which included testing the rockets and different orbital and lunar modules in orbit. In fact, it wasn't until Apollo 8 that a manned vehicle was sent towards the Moon and back, and before that mission, the most famous Apollo mission was Apollo 1, albeit for all the wrong reasons.

There were no delusions regarding the dangers of manned space travel, but they were brought home on January 27, 1967, when all three astronauts were killed by a fire that ignited in the cabin during a launch rehearsal. To this day, there is still debate over what ignited the fire, but the disaster made clear that the modules being used by NASA had a series of fatal flaws. After the Apollo 1 tragedy, NASA changed its plans by first running a series of unmanned missions to test the Saturn rockets and the different modules throughout 1967 and early 1968. and it would not be until Apollo 7 launched about 20 months after the disaster that NASA dared to conduct another manned mission.

Apollo 1 and the Space Shuttle Challenger: The History of NASA's Two Most Notorious Disasters analyzes the conception of the Apollo program and the events that brought about the fateful disaster. Along with pictures of important people, places, and events, you will learn about Apollo 1 like never before.

The *Challenger* Disaster

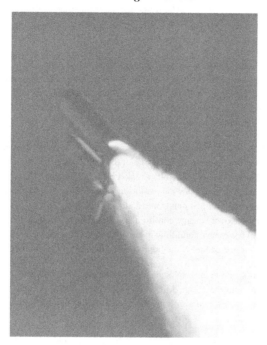

A Picture of the *Challenger* 58 seconds into its final mission

In the decades after the Apollo program, American space shuttles flew over 130 missions and successfully completed over 98% of them, but unfortunately, the two most famous missions were the ones that ended tragically aboard the *Challenger* and *Columbia*.

The Space Shuttle *Challenger* was the most heavily used space shuttle in the three years it was operational, carrying the first minority astronaut and woman astronaut into space. *Challenger* was also the first space shuttle to complete a landing at night.

On the morning of January 28, 1986, the Space Shuttle *Challenger* launched for the 10th time, beginning mission STS-51-L. Space shuttles had already successfully completed 24 missions, and no American spacecraft had ever failed to reach orbit during an official mission. On this mission, the *Challenger* was carrying a satellite for the Tracking and Data Relay Satellites system, which was to be deployed in orbit. The crew included Ronald McNair, who had already been the second African-American in space, and Ellison Onizuka, who had already been the first

Asian-American astronaut in space. But the highlight of the mission was to be the "NASA Teacher in Space Project," in which a civilian teacher would give teaching lessons to his or her class while onboard the space shuttle. The winner of the competition was Christa McAuliffe, a high school teacher in Concord, New Hampshire, who wrote a winning essay and had to undergo a year of astronaut training before that fateful day.

It was a beautiful morning, and many spectators came to the Kennedy Space Center to watch the launch, including McAuliffe's parents and her students. Several news networks were carrying live broadcasts of the launch, including live shots of McAuliffe's parents as they watched the *Challenger* liftoff. Mission Control's transmissions to the *Challenger* were being blared over loudspeakers to give spectators a play-by-play of the shuttle's ascent.

Ascent seemed to be going normally during the first minute, but about 75 seconds into the ascent, a plastic O-ring used to seal a joint in one of the solid rocket boosters failed, causing a breach of hot gas. That gas spread to the other rocket booster and the external fuel tank, causing an explosion. When the spectators saw the explosion, many of them started cheering, unaware of what was really happening. But Mission Control quickly announced that there had been some sort of problem, and the crowd became confused and then panicky as the space shuttle, fuel tank and rocket boosters all broke apart and flew in opposite directions. Some cameras fixed on the falling debris as it fell to the ocean, while others stayed focused on McAuliffe's parents.

The entire crew was killed in the explosion, and investigations concluded that they may have survived until crashing into the ocean. After the *Challenger* disaster, the space shuttles were grounded for about two years, and a commission issued findings that would be used in an effort to prevent similar tragedies.

Apollo 1 and the Space Shuttle Challenger: The History of NASA's Two Most Notorious Disasters chronicles the disaster from the origins of its mission to what went so terribly wrong. Along with pictures of important people, places, and events, you will learn about the *Challenger* like never before.

Apollo 1

Chapter 1: A Great New American Enterprise

"Now it is time to take longer strides - time for a great new American enterprise - time for this nation to take a clearly leading role in space achievement, which in many ways may hold the key to our future on Earth." – President Kennedy, 1961

A picture of Kennedy's address to Congress in 1961

The Apollo missions would require cutting edge rockets to launch state of the art modular spacecrafts to the Moon, while ensuring a successful reentry of the spacecraft back into Earth's atmosphere. When Kennedy outlined the vision in 1961, NASA did not yet possess the scientific or technological know-how for the spacecraft's return, and the spacecraft and rockets themselves did not exist yet.

At the beginning of the Apollo program, NASA wasn't even sure what the design would be for the spacecraft that would go to the Moon and back. At first blush, NASA's engineers assumed it would be easiest to directly launch a spacecraft to the Moon and equip it with boosters to launch it back to Earth. This approach, referred to as "direct ascent," seemed feasible to NASA because the Moon had no atmosphere, making ascent from the Moon relatively easy.

Still, a minority of NASA employees advocated other designs. One design, known as "Earth Orbit Rendezvous," would have attempted to assemble several pieces together into a spacecraft while in orbit. The "Earth Orbit Rendezvous" was used to assemble the International Space

Station, but it was beyond the capabilities of NASA in the 1960s.

Meanwhile, another minority advocated what came to be known as the "Lunar Orbit Rendezvous" mission. Lunar Orbit Rendezvous required having a rocket launch a spacecraft consisting of three major components: a service module, command module and lunar module. The three modules would remain attached until the spacecraft began orbiting the Moon, at which point the lunar module detached and landed on the surface while the Command/service module orbited the Moon. The advocates for this type of mission argued that it would actually be the best option because it would require landing the least mass on the Moon. By the end of 1962, NASA was convinced that a Lunar Orbit Rendezvous mission was the best option.

Once NASA settled on using Lunar Orbit Rendezvous for the Apollo missions, they still had to design and construct the modular spacecraft and rockets. Right away, NASA faced a major logistical challenge; any lunar landing mission would require multiple crewmembers, but NASA had never developed a spacecraft that held more than one crewmember. To accomplish this, NASA designed a Command/service module. The service module would hold essentials like oxygen, water, and power, while the three astronauts would be in the command module during liftoff, orbit and reentry. The ultra-light lunar module, which was designed to descend and ascend to and from the Moon, could hold two astronauts. On ascent from the Moon, the lunar module would re-dock with the still orbiting Command/service module.

Designing the spacecraft wasn't even the hardest part. NASA also had to develop rockets capable of first launching the modular spacecraft into Earth's orbit, and then launching it toward the Moon. The Soviets struggled throughout the 1960s to design rockets up to the task, but NASA got it right with the Saturn V rocket, which to this day remains the most powerful launching rocket NASA ever used.

The Saturn V rocket ahead of the launch of Apollo 10

The Saturn V rockets were truly gargantuan, standing nearly 350 feet tall and holding thousands of tons of fuel. These rockets could carry a payload weighing over 250,000 pounds into orbit, giving it the ability to launch the Apollo spacecraft into orbit in about 12 minutes at nearly 18,000 miles per hour. But that was just the beginning of the Saturn V's duties. Once in orbit, the Saturn V still had to accelerate the spacecraft to nearly 25,000 miles per hour to allow the spacecraft to escape the Earth's orbit and head for the Moon.

Designing rocket engines that powerful was hard enough, but NASA had to design the Saturn V to accomplish its duties in multiple stages, because an Apollo spacecraft typically had to spend a few hours in orbit around the Earth before heading for the Moon. Thus, the Saturn V's first two stages would accelerate the spacecraft to about 15,000 miles per hour, while the third and final stage would enter the spacecraft into Earth's orbit at about 18,000 miles per hour. But this third and final stage also had to be capable of essentially restarting and reaccelerating to propel the spacecraft out of Earth's orbit and to the Moon at about 25,000 miles per hour.

The first challenge was to get the Apollo spacecraft into orbit, which required escaping Earth's atmosphere at about 18,000 miles per hour. From the launch pad, the first stage of the Saturn V rocket would accelerate the spacecraft to over 6,000 miles per hour in two and a half minutes before detaching and falling away. The second stage accelerated the spacecraft to about 15,000 miles per hour after six more minutes before falling away.

The Saturn V's third stage was the most crucial. First, it accelerated the spacecraft to 18,000 to enter it into orbit before shutting down. The spacecraft then orbited around the Earth to wait for the Moon's orbit to properly line up for the three day voyage to the Moon's orbit. The Apollo spacecrafts usually had to orbit around Earth at least once before it was time to head to the Moon. At the speed the spacecraft was going, it would only take a few hours to orbit the entire planet.

Next, the Saturn V's third stage had to reactivate itself for the "Trans Lunar Injection," accelerating the spacecraft to about 25,000 miles per hour to reach the escape velocity necessary to escape Earth's orbit. At this time, the lunar module attached to the command/service module, and once the spacecraft reached escape velocity, the Saturn V's third stage fell away on a different trajectory.

Once the spacecraft escaped Earth's orbit, it would take three days of cruising and a short engine burst known as the "Lunar Orbit Insertion" procedure to properly position the spacecraft to be captured by the Moon's orbit. NASA had mapped the Moon during previous missions, in order to help choose the landing sites for the Apollo lunar modules. When the Moon captured the spacecraft, the spacecraft would complete several orbits around the Moon to properly line up the lunar module for descent.

To descend thousands of feet down to the Moon's surface, the lunar module had both an engine and thrusters that would allow it to maintain speed, control and direction. The lunar module would descend in a pirouette to help it descend straight. As Apollo 11's lunar module inadvertently proved, any incorrect timing or ill timed thrust would land a module several miles away from its intended destination, which could be the difference between a smooth landing or landing among boulders and craters. For most of the descent, the lunar module was automated, but the final stage of the descent required manual controls. When the descent stage was finished, it would fall away from the module, like the Saturn V rocket stages.

The Apollo astronauts usually spent between 20-36 hours on the Moon's surface, collecting several pounds of rocks and samples, and in later missions using rovers to travel around. When it was time to leave the Moon's surface, the lunar module would ascend back to re-dock with the command/service module. Since the Moon has no atmosphere, it was relatively easy for the lunar modules to ascend without needing powerful rockets like the Saturn V. The lunar module had an ascent stage with fuel propulsion engines to propel it back up to the command/service module. Once the lunar module rejoined the orbiter, the ascent stage was jettisoned, often landing back on the Moon.

The Moon's orbit is only a fraction of Earth's, so once the modules linked back up, the Command/service module was equipped with engines to propel it back toward Earth. The bigger concern for the return was that the modules had to reenter Earth's orbit at the proper angle to allow the planet to recapture it. Reentry into Earth's atmosphere subjects spacecrafts to temperatures of about 3,000 degrees Fahrenheit, so the module had an elaborate heat shield consisting of a mixture of dozens of panels, insulation and aluminum. A failure in any part of the heat shield system would be fatal.

Finally, it was time for the splashdown. The module had several "drogue parachutes," used for decelerating fast moving objects, which were used at about 25,000 feet. Those parachutes slowed the module down to about 125 miles per hour. Another set of parachutes would then slow the module down to about 20 miles per hour before it hit the water.

Once the module splashed down, divers would deploy rafts to pick up the astronauts and anchor the module while a helicopter hovered overhead to collect everyone and everything. After being picked up, the returning astronauts would be quarantined for a period of time to study the effects the mission had on their bodies.

A picture of the Apollo 1 crew practicing the splashdown and exiting the module

Most people can name Apollo 11 as the first mission to land men on the Moon, and a critically acclaimed film about Apollo 13's harrowing mission was released in 1995. As a result, the rest of the Apollo missions have been greatly overshadowed, including Apollo 8, despite the fact Apollo 8 accomplished several firsts and ultimately made Apollo 11 possible. However, none of those missions would've taken place the way they did without the bitter lessons learned by Apollo 1.

Cape Canaveral Air Force Station Launch Complex 34, site of the Apollo 1 disaster

Chapter 2: Simulated Launch

Picture of the arrival of the Apollo 1 command module

"On the morning of January 27, 1967, a test of SIC 012 commenced. The purpose of the test was to verify systems operation in a simulated launch and to exercise countdown procedures in preparation for actual launch. The test was identified as a Space Vehicle Plugs Out Integrated Test OCP FO-K-0021-1 in which the spacecraft would be electrically disconnected from the Ground Support Equipment (GSE) by removing the umbilical connectors normally disconnected at the time of launch." – Passage from the *Report of the Apollo 204 Review Board*

In a nation that was becoming increasingly bogged down in Vietnam and where Civil Rights marchers and leaders were regularly targeted for violence, the space program had become for many a shining beacon, giving hope to a nation in desperate need of something to believe in. Just a few days before the Apollo 1 disaster, a *United Press International* article had announced, "Apollo 1 astronauts Virgil (Gus) Grissom, Edward White and Roger Chaffee are set to ride a powerful Saturn rocket into orbit Feb. 21 to inaugurate the manned portion of the Apollo men-to-the-moon program. The launch date, made official Monday by the U.S. Space Agency, misses by one day the fifth anniversary of America's first orbital venture—the 5 1-2 hour flight of John Glenn in the 'Friendship 7' Mercury capsule."

White, Grissom, and Chafee posing with a model of the Command/service module

A picture of the Apollo 1 crew and the backup crew: David R. Scott, James A. McDivitt, and Russell L. Schweickart

Known officially as AS-204, the Apollo 1 spacecraft was designed to be the first manned Command/service Module to orbit the earth for any length of time, perhaps as much as two weeks, and the confidence that both NASA and the American people had in the program could be seen in the *Command Service Module System Handbook*, published less than two weeks before the incident. According to that publication, the module had "been prepared by the Flight Control Division, Manned Spacecraft Center, Houston, Texas, with technical support by North American Aviation" and contained the following stern warning: "Information contained within this section represents the Command Service Module Systems for the AS-501 Mission as of January 16, 1967. Information as shown reflects spacecraft systems with major emphasis on material for use by Flight Controllers in real time; however, caution should be exercised in using these systems drawings for any purpose other than flight control." Ironically, although it was more than 300 pages long, it contained no information on emergency exit systems for the module.

The three men who were part of the launch rehearsal that day knew full well the potential danger of the mission and even mockingly prayed to a model of their command/service module in one parody of their official mission portrait. The commander of the mission was Virgil Grissom, known to his friends and the American public as Gus, and when asked about the danger of space travel a month before the disaster, he replied, "You sort of have to put that out of your mind. There's always a possibility that you can have a catastrophic failure, of course; this can happen on any flight; it can happen on the last one as well as the first one. So, you just plan as best you can to take care of all these eventualities, and you get a well-trained crew and you go fly." After his death, one Associated Press article observed, "For Air Force Lt. Col. Virgil I. Grissom, the first Apollo mission would have been his third trip into space, a distinction no man today can claim. ... Some called Gus Grissom a hard-luck astronaut. As one of the famed original seven Mercury spacemen, he became the second American to fly in space. Taking a 15-minute sub-orbital flight July 21, 1961 he had to swim for his life when his tiny spaceship, Liberty Bell 7, blew its hatch and sank. On March 23, 1965, he and Navy Cmdr. John W. Young had the honor of launching the United States into its highly successful Gemini program with a three-orbit flight in Gemini 3. Grissom, 40, was a short man with a deep, business-like voice who wore his hair in a crewcut. Born in Mitchell, Ind., he once said he decided as a sixth grader there, watching airplanes overhead, that the flying business was for him. The Air Force turned him down because he was too young, only 17, when he first tried to enlist as a fighter pilot in World War II. He got on duty a year later, but as a typist. He married his high school sweetheart, Betty Moore, during his first leave. After the war he worked as a fry cook in a hamburger shop, while his wife worked as a telephone operator, and graduated from Purdue University. During the Korean War he finally won his wings, going on to fly 100 missions and win the Distinguished Flying Cross. He became an astronaut in 1959."

With Grissom on that fateful morning were Edward White and Roger Chaffee. Of White, the same reporter wrote, "The son of an Air Force General, White, 36, was born in San Antonio, Tex., but lived there only a short time. As a 'military brat' he was at a loss to call any place his home town. He was graduated from West Point and later earned a master's degree in aeronautical engineering from the University of Michigan. Still later he attended test pilot school at Edwards Air Force Base, Calif. A deeply religious man, White, a Methodist, attended church regularly. He kept his six-foot frame in top physical condition. In fact, he ranked No. 1 in physical aptitude in his class of 1952 at West Point, and set a 440-yard hurdle record. He married the former Patricia E. Finegan of Washington D.C., and they had a son and a daughter."

According to the article, Chaffee was born to be a pilot and "inherited his love for the air. His father, Donald Chaffee of Grand Rapids, Mich., is a former barnstormer who flew at county fairs in an open cockpit airplane. The astronaut was slight, dark-haired man who at 31 already had begun to gray. Coworkers praised him as a smart engineer. ... Chaffee held a bachelor's degree in aeronautical engineering from Purdue and chose a Navy career through the ROTC program. He met his wife, Martha Horn of Oklahoma City, Okla., while at Purdue. Chaffee became an astronaut with the third group named in 1963 after a tour of duty at the Jacksonville, Fla., Naval Air Station. Part of his duty there was taking pictures of Mercury Spaceships as they soared aloft from Cape Kennedy, Fla."

A picture of the men pretending to pray to the module

The nation had much to look forward to with this latest venture, as Apollo 1 would carry a television camera, designed to send video back to NASA and to let the astronauts broadcast portions of their flight to audiences on earth. This was a vital part of NASA's public relations campaign to keep their very expensive budget intact. As the Vietnam War continued to heat up and the War on Poverty became a popular cause, some in the country were beginning to question why the government was spending so much money to send a few men into space.

Chapter 3: The Plugs-Out Test

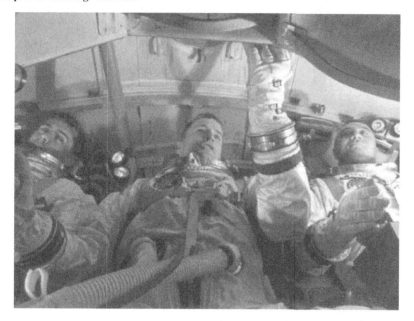

A picture of the crew training in a simulator

A picture of the crew entering the module in a previous test in 1966

"The Plugs-Out Test was initiated on January 27, 1967 at 12:55 GMT (7:55 a.m. EST) when power was applied to the spacecraft for this test. After completion of initial verification tests of system operation the flight crew entered the Command Module. ... The Command Pilot noted an odor in the Spacecraft Environmental Control System suit oxygen loop and the count was held at 18:20 GMT while a sample of the oxygen in this system was taken. This odor has been determined from subsequent analysis not to be related to the fire. ... Communication difficulties were encountered and the count was held at approximately 22:40 GMT to troubleshoot the problem. ... From 22:45 GMT until about 22:53 GMT the flight crew interchanged equipment related to the communications systems in an effort to isolate the communications system problem. ... During the troubleshooting period problems developed in the ability of various ground stations to communicate with one another and with the crew. None of the communications problems appear to have had a direct bearing on the fire." – Passage from the *Report of the Apollo 204 Review Board*

Entering 1967, the Apollo project was going well. In fact, during the previous month, NASA had decided to cancel one of its major test flights, ruling that such an expensive trip was not needed. Instead, the three man crew could focus on preparing for their February 21 launch.

On the fateful morning of January 27, they were performing the Plugs Out Integrated Test. According to the report of the Apollo 204 Review Board, "The purpose of the Space Vehicle Plugs-Out Integrated Test, Operational Checkout Procedures (OCP) FO-K-0021-1, Spacecraft 012 is to demonstrate all space vehicle systems and operational procedures in as near a flight configuration as is practical and to verify their capability in a simulated launch. System verification is performed, an abbreviated final countdown conducted and a flight simulation made. All communication and instrumentation systems are activated and proper measurements are monitored at appropriate ground stations. At the start of the simulated flight, umbilicals are disconnected and the spacecraft is on simulated fuel-cell power. Specific objectives of this test for Spacecraft 012 as stated in the Final Procedure Document were:

a) To verify overall spacecraft/launch vehicle compatibility and demonstrate proper function of spacecraft systems with all umbilicals and Ground Support Equipment disconnected.

b) To verify no electrical interference at the time of umbilical disconnect.

c) To verify astronaut emergency egress procedures (unaided egress) at the conclusion of the test."

At first, everything seemed to be functioning normally. The test began at 7:55 a.m., but when the astronauts entered the module and took their seats around 1:00 p.m., Grissom complained about smelling a strange odor that he described as a "sour smell" coming from his oxygen supply. This resulted in the simulated countdown being stopped at 1:20, but after checking it out, the men in charge determined that it was nothing to be concerned about and authorized the tests to continue. The countdown started again around 2:45 in the afternoon. When the countdown resumed, support crew stepped forward to secure the three hatches which would ultimately trap the crew in the sudden inferno.

Lewis Curatolo, from North American Aviation, helped the astronauts into their seats that fateful day and later reported, "At approximately 1300 I notified the Test Conductor and Test Project Engineer that we were ready to perform Crew ingress. The Suit Technician and the Spacecraft Technician performed the pre-ingress layout of the cockpit and couches. This procedure consists of laying out the pilots seat and shoulder harnesses, and routing of the 02 umbilical hoses. ... After completion of the Crew ingress we proceeded with Hatch closeout, and Cabin purge, as directed by the Environmental Control System engineer and Test Project Engineer. ... At this time we were directed to proceed with outer hatch and Boost Protective Cover closeout. We installed the outer crew hatch and started with the Boost Protective Cover installation but experienced some difficulty in getting the Boost Protective Cover to lock in, so I notified the Test Project Engineer and asked for an Interim Discrepancy Report. The Boost Protective Cover was left unlatched and we were instructed by the Test Supervisor and Test Conductor to clear the White Room. I followed the Test Conductor's instructions and at this point (1730) the 2nd shift Pad Leader (Don Babbitt) relieved me."

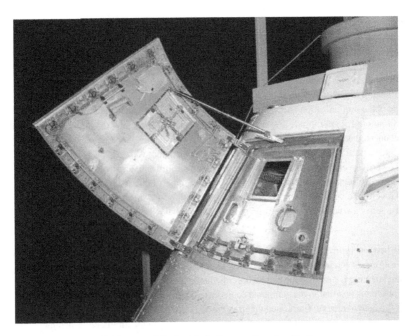

A picture of the hatch design used on Apollo 1

As if there hadn't been enough omens, the countdown had to be stopped again at 5:40 due to communication problems. The crew was wired with a live microphone that they needed to be able to turn off from time to time, but the microphone could not be turned off. While this problem was being dealt with, other activities related to the countdown continued, and at 6:20 p.m., with all other countdown functions completed, NASA decided to hold the launch clock at T-10 until the problem with the microphone could be fixed.

As much as investigators looked back again and again at the crew's final moments, no one could ever determine what exactly went wrong. The Review Board later noted, "From the start of the T-10 minute hold at 23:20 GMT until about 23:30 GMT there are no events that appear to be related to the fire. The major activity during this period was routine troubleshooting of the communications problem. The records show that except for the communications problem, all systems were operating normally during this period. There were no voice transmissions from the spacecraft from 23:30:14 GMT until the transmission reporting the fire which began at 23:31:04.7 GMT (6:31:04.7 p.m. EST)."

As far as what was going on inside the module or in the heads of those who were unwittingly facing imminent death, there is no evidence to indicate that they had any concerns. NASA took the health of its astronauts seriously and wired them with numerous sensors designed to immediately detect any sort of physical problem that might compromise the mission. Not only did these monitors constantly transmit data back to Mission Control, they also left behind records that showed how the men were doing. According to those who examined these records, "During the period beginning about 30 seconds before the report there are indications of crew movement. ... There is, however, no evidence as to what this crew movement was or that it was related to the fire. The biomedical data indicate that just prior to the fire report the Senior Pilot was performing essentially no activity (or was in the baseline 'rest' condition) until about 23:30:21 GMT [6:30:21 locally] when a slight increase in pulse and respiratory rate was noted. At 23:30:30 GMT the electrocardiogram indicates some muscular activity for several seconds. Similar indications are noted at 23:30:39 GMT. The data show increased activity but are not indicative of an alarm type of response. By 23:30:45 GMT, all of the biomedical parameters had reverted to the baseline 'rest' level."

Another sensor that registered movement was the gas chromatograph cable, which would have run to the gas chromatograph had it been installed in the command module. According to the report, "When the gas chromatograph is not connected, the cable acts as an antenna. Thus, changes in the electromagnetic field within the spacecraft are sensed when the cable is approached closely, touched or moved or voltage fluctuations occur in other equipment. Variations found in the signal level from the gas chromatograph cable at earlier times in the test have been correlated with either crew movement or voltage transients when equipment was turned off or on at these earlier times. The variation at 23:30:50 GMT, may have resulted because it was touched or approached by the crew since there does not appear to be any voltage transient condition at this time which could have given the observed signal."

In essence, investigators could find nothing in the data to indicate at that point in time that the astronauts of Apollo 1 had only seconds to live.

Chapter 4: A Flash Fire

"Gus Grissom, Edward White and Roger Chaffee were killed tonight in a flash fire during tests of the Apollo Saturn 204 vehicle at Cape Kennedy AFB. The fire occurred while the astronauts were in the space craft during the countdown of simulated flight test. The accident occurred at 6:31 EST at T-10 minutes prior to the planned simulated liftoff. The spacecraft was located 218 feet above the launch pad and was mated to the uprated Saturn 1B launch vehicle. Hatches on the spacecraft were closed. Emergency crews were hampered by dense smoke removing the hatches. An unknown number of launch crew workers were treated to smoke inhalation at the Cape Kennedy dispensary. The crew had entered the spacecraft at 3 p.m. Minor difficulties had been encountered during the count with the environmental control and communications systems. All data has been impounded pending an investigation." - Official statement from NASA following the accident

Perhaps the only positive thing that can be said about the tragedy was that when the end came, it likely happened very quickly. At 6:30:54.8 local time, the machines monitoring the module noted "a significant voltage transient" in the AC Bus 2 voltage, and 10 seconds later, the men indicated there was a problem. 30 seconds after that, they were likely dead, or at least unconscious.

The tape recordings made from the astronaut's microphones show that they likely suffered for only a few seconds, though how long that time period seemed to be to them is beyond human imagination. According to an analysis made of the tapes:

"The total time duration of these two transmissions was brief, lasting 17.1 seconds; the first lasted 5.3 seconds and the second lasted 5.0 seconds, with a 6.8 second period of no transmission between... Except for a portion of the first transmission, which is quite clear, the remainder of the first and second transmission is not clear and it is impossible to define exactly what was said by the crew. ... [The first] transmission began at 23:31:04.7 GMT [6:31:04.7 local time] with an exclamatory remark. ... Most listeners believe this initial remark was one of the following: 'Hey ' 'Fire ' 'Break ' Most listeners believe...that this transmission was made by the Command Pilot. This remark is followed by a short period of noise (bumping sounds, etc.). ... The second portion of this first transmission begins at 23:31:06.2 GMT with an unclear word. Most listeners believe the first to be one of the following: 'I 've' 'We've' The remainder of this transmission is quite clear and is: '...Got a fire in the cockpit', followed by a clipped word sounding like 'VHEH', which ended at 23:31:10 GMT. Many listeners believed this transmission to have been made by the Pilot. ... The entire second transmission is somewhat garbled [and] is subject to wide variation of... The following is a list of some of the interpretations that have been made:

(1). 'Fighting a bad fire - Let's get out ..... Open 'er up.'

(2). 'We've got a bad fire - Let's get out ..... We're burning up. ' 'I'm reporting a bad fire .... I'm getting out..Oh, AAH.' (Scream)"

A. R. Caswell, who was at one of the television monitors, later testified, "At approximately 18:30 Eastern Standard Time my attention was directed to the monitor by OTV technician Gary Propst, his remarks was that there is a fire in the capsule. ... Upon directing my attention to the remark by technician Propst, I observed on the white room camera, a flickering of flame inside of the capsule on the left side of the port hole. This flame flickered for some time I would estimate 15 - 20 seconds and then it spread across almost the full face of the port in the hatch cover. ... Reverting my glance back again to the camera covering the hatch porthole I would estimate that some 30 to 40 seconds elapsed before the flames reached a very high proportion, in which there was nothing visible but a white searing type of flame inside the cockpit. The period specified from 15 to, or rather to, 30 to 40 seconds was subsequent to my initial time that I observed the fire in the hatch. The fire, the flames that I saw were definitely inside the capsule, there was no fire around the hatch at this particular point in time."

The men had trained for such an emergency and seem to have sprung into action to try to survive. The protocol called for White, occupying the center seat, to unlatch the inner hatch, and video recorded by the television camera gave the impression that he at least tried to do this. Caswell testified, that "when we first noticed the flames at the cockpit it appeared on the left side facing the hatch cover. And it was during this initial period that we detected what we feel was motion by some movement of the helmet of the center crew member. And then seconds perhaps 10 to 15 seconds the flames had spread across the face. ...I did notice what appeared to be motion of the center crew man upon the initial outbreak of fire as my observation was directed to it. And then it appeared within perhaps 20 seconds, the flames had obscured a good view or any type of view of the crew member because they were spread across the face of the porthole. As time progressed, perhaps to 45 seconds to a minute, the intensity of the flames greatly increased to where they appeared to be white hot. This is confined to inside the spacecraft."

One thing that has troubled investigators for years is the testimony of Propst, who also watched on his video monitor as events unfolded but gave a very different time line. According to Propst, "At about 1830 one of the Astronauts said, 'Fire in the cockpit', this was followed by a scream and then silence. ... Immediately I looked over to our camera 24 which is located inside the White Room. ...as soon as my eyes caught sight of the camera 24 monitor I noticed a bright glow inside the spacecraft, however, I saw no flames. Just a split second later I saw flames go past the porthole. The flames were not in the order of an explosion but were, in fact, that of something just burning. The fire increased steadily during the next two to two and one half minutes. ... The first thing I saw was what appeared to be the center Astronaut's arms reaching above his head toward the hatch. There followed a great deal of motion as his arms seemed to fumble with something and then quickly reach back for it. From time to time the top of his helmet could be seen. About 15 seconds after the cry of fire, I saw more arms in front of the porthole seemingly coming from the left. Looking further back into the spacecraft, I could see the legs of the center Astronaut moving about. The movement inside the spacecraft lasted about 2 minutes before the flames began to block the view. At first the flames were behind the Astronaut's arms toward the center of the spacecraft and then spread forward to the area of the hatch."

As they watched the scene unfold, Propst and his co-workers speculated about exactly what they were seeing, trying as people so often do during a disaster to wrap their minds around an incredible and unbelievable situation. He continued, "During the entire time that I watched the Astronauts' moving, their spacesuits were silver in color with no signs of being burned or charred. I think it noteworthy that no one entered the White Room until it had become smoke-filled some minutes later. Had anyone entered and gone near the spacecraft they would have been visible on the TV camera. ... I know that my times are very near accurate because I remember saying to others that had gathered in the area of the monitor: 'Blow the hatch, why don't they blow the hatch?' One person that was near said that the spacesuits would protect them from the heat until they could get out. A short conversation then took place concerning how long and how much the suits could protect them from the fire. Also comment was made on why no one had entered the White Room as yet. During the time of this conversation the White Room was still clear and the Astronaut's motion still visible."

Chapter 5: The Hatch Fell

"Gleaves who had at various times been forced to the swing arm by the smoke, returned, saw that the hatch was part way down and gave it a kick. As a result of the kick, the hatch fell even further into the Command Module. Gleaves had secured a flashlight from his tool box during one of his entries into the white room and peered into the dark smoke and soot-covered interior of the Command Module. He could see nothing except the faint glow of the floodlights mounted near the couches. The lights were within inches of his position, but they appeared to be small candles very far away. W. M. Medcalf entered the 'white room' and began his attempt to remove the inner hatch completely from the Command Module. Members of the regular fire department began arriving at Level A-8. The pad egress team, which had been standing by at the fire station, also responded to the call, but in much slower M113 Armored Personnel Carriers. The team was scheduled to participate in the egress exercise, scheduled at the end of the plugs out test." – Passage from the *Report of the Apollo 204 Review Board*

Since White likely passed out before he could open the hatch, it was left to those on the outside to try to conduct a rescue, but they were plagued with problems that prevented them from offering any timely help. When investigators asked how much time actually passed before the astronauts were reached, Donald Babbitt of North American Aviation testified to the Review Board, "The time period in here I can only estimate as 5 to 15 seconds. I heard on the head set…Mr. Chaffee say, 'There is a fire in here,' (or words to this effect). I ordered the mechanical lead man, Mr. Gleaves, to 'Get them out of there' (meaning remove the hatches and get the crew out of the Command Module)."

However, less than 20 seconds after the fire in the module broke out, the flame breached its exterior and began to spread. At this point, Babbitt realized that his own life was in danger because if the fire spread out of control, it might reach the rocket fuel and cause a detonation that would've leveled the entire launch pad. He recalled, "I started to turn toward the Communications Box (on my left), when out of the corner of my eye, I saw flame come out from under the boost near the steam duct. I almost completed my turn when I was hit by a concussion or sheet of flame (I don't remember hearing an explosion) and was pushed toward the communication boxes. My next thoughts were to get out of there. (I never had time to notify the blockhouse). I went to the umbilical (White Room) arm, [into which the hatch should open] and went across it to the umbilical tower where I encountered three of the spacecraft mechanics and an elevator talker who had a head set. I told the talker to inform the test supervisor that we were on fire and that I need firemen, ambulances, and equipment. With the three mechanics (Messrs. Gleaves, Hawkins, and Clemmons) we grabbed the only C02 bottle available and went back to the White Room to try to remove the hatches. The smoke and heat was so intense that we could only spend a short time in the White Room (possibly 1-2 minutes). After several trips back and forth Mr. Gleaves almost passed out due to smoke inhalation so I ordered him to stay out, which he did but for only a short time."

Pictures of the charred module

Crises, especially when being handled by highly trained personnel, typically begin as a highly structured and detail-oriented exercise but often progress to more and more desperate measures, as the best trained among the respondents exchange procedures for experience and initiative. So it was in the minutes that followed the Apollo 1 fire. James Gleaves, one of the first men to approach the module, later reported that "a gentleman named L. D. Reece found the oxygen masks and was handing out the oxygen masks. We had trouble locating the strip of tape on the bottom because they were painted the same color as the connector. And several times, one, two, three or four of us returned without masks and stayed as long as we could, then finally Babbitt and myself entered the white room after the fire had been extinguished by Jerry Hawkins and on all fours I crawled. I found the tool to remove the ablative hatch. I removed the ablative hatch and I didn't have a mask on at this time and I just couldn't take it no longer so I returned out and gave the tool to Jerry Hawkins, Steve Clements and L. D. Reece. And they removed the ablative hatch and L. D. Reece threw it out on level A8 and then these guys, also they had masks on, they removed the inner hatch and it was so hot they just let it drop down under the couch. So they come back out and I in return went in and kicked the inner hatch and it sort of fell down under the couch. I pushed but it was still hot and inside the spacecraft was black and filled full of smoke. You couldn't see anything at all. So I returned to A8 and out of the white room and got a flashlight and went back in and tried to see inside the spacecraft but the heat was too great and the smoke was too bad so we returned out on A8 and we continued to go back in. And as far as I can remember it took maybe 10 or 15 minutes for any fireman or any help to get to us up on the swing arm."

Within a few minutes, the fire nearest the module was under control, and Babbitt was placed in the unenviable position of opening the hatches. Babbitt was perhaps the first person to understand that due to a flawed design that would be discussed for decades, the men trapped inside never really had a chance of escape. Due to the increase in pressure inside the cabin during the fire, the hatches would never have been able to fully open. Babbitt recalled, "After the smoke had cleared some, I could see that the Spacecraft Technicians and Quality Control (NASA and NAA) had been able to get back into level A-8 and were fighting fires with everything available, so I got some more men and continued as best we could (because of the smoke and heat) to remove the hatches. We attempted to both remove the inner hatch or lower the hatch down inside the Command Module. We were not successful in removing the inner hatch and could only lower the hatch about 75 to 80% of the way because of obstructions. I was at that time only able, again because of the smoke which was considerable, to observe only two of the flight crew but could not recognize who it was. The inner hatch was extremely hot and we could only handle it with the handles attached to the hatch. My observation at the time of hatch removal was that the flight crew were dead and that the destruction inside the Command Module was considerable."

There was little he could now do for the men who only moments before had been his co-workers, but Babbitt carried on with his duty before finally succumbing to his own injuries. "After informing the test supervisor of what I had observed (while adhering to security guidelines wherever possible) and continued to direct the crew in putting out the fires. I asked the senior Pan American firemen to specifically check the Launch Escape Motor for hot spots and general heat. I was relieved by Mr. Curatolo, NAA 1st shift pad leader. I proceeded down the umbilical tower elevator, met the two NASA doctors and briefed them on what they would find. I then proceeded to the Pan American Dispensary, with a short stop at the NAA Shop Trailer, for treatment and checkup. I was treated for smoke inhalation, flash burns, and eye irritation, and ordered to remain overnight."

On February 8, Babbitt was called back to testify as to what he observed when he opened the hatch. He described the gruesome scene in vivid detail:

"When the inner hatch was first lowered, the only thing that I could observe was smoke inside. We could only feel the flight crew. We could not see them very well as I could tell. As the men working with me went out because they'd been in the smoke quite a while, I went back in, oh, approximately one minute or a minute and a half later; and all that I could observe was what appeared to be Mr. White laying on his back with his arms over his head, appeared to be reaching for the hatch or in something in that vicinity. I also observed what appeared to be Mr. Grissom laying with one of his arms through and appeared to be reaching in the direction of the hatch also.

I went out again for a short bit and came back in maybe thirty seconds after that. I could see a little bit more. The smoke had cleared some more. All that I could really see was, oh maybe, to the waist of Mr. White. ... I at first got the impression that they were off the seats; and then I got the impression that no they were on the seats. It appeared that their suits were shredded. I could see bare skin. ... The crew appeared to me to be in their normal, in-flight position. I could only see what appeared to be Mr. Grissom's left arm reaching through Mr. White's arm. I could not see his body that well, but it had the appearance of being in its satisfactory or its normal position. I did not observe Mr. Chaffee because I was a little bit too far to the right of the hatch and could not see him. Mr. White appeared to me to be as I say, laying in his normal boost position. I could not tell whether his head rest was up or down. In fact, I couldn't even see his features because of the, what appeared the smoke or soot blackened face plate on his helmet."

Lewis Curatolo, who had earlier helped the men into their seats and himself helped seal the hatches, recalled, "I observed that the body of the Senior Pilot was wedged between the Crew Couches and the hatch bulkhead; the Command Pilot was positioned in the center couch with his body partially hanging over the center couch. The Pilot was in a reclining position in the Pilot's Couch. I observed that the Command Pilot's leg pans were in the rest position, the Senior Pilot's leg pans were in the boost position, and the Pilot's leg pans were in the full down position."

Chapter 6: The Fire Department

"Shortly after the report of fire, a call was made to the fire department. From log records, it appears that the fire apparatus and personnel were dispatched at about 23:32 GMT. After hearing the report of the fire, the doctor monitoring the test from the blockhouse near the pad proceeded to the base of the umbilical tower. The exact time at which firemen reached Level A-8 is not known. Personnel who opened the hatches unanimously state that all hatches were open before any firemen were seen on the level or in the White Room. The first firemen who reached Level A-8 state that all hatches were open, but that the inner hatch was inside the Command Module, when they arrived. This places arrival of the firemen after 23:36 GMT. It is estimated, on the basis of tests, that seven to eight minutes were required to travel from the fire station to the launch complex and to ride the elevator from the ground to Level A-8. Thus, the estimated time of firemen arrival at level A-8 is shortly before 23:40 GMT." – Passage from the *Report of the Apollo 204 Review Board*

James Burch was one of the firemen sent over that evening, and with the fire already extinguished, their first priority was to try to rescue the astronauts. He later testified, "From the time we received the call, I would estimate that we got to the gantry in around five or six minutes. We took the slow elevator up. The fast elevator was out. It took us approximately two minutes to reach the top of the gantry. Assistant Chief, McMillan, Bob Batts the Crew Chief, Rector - Fire Fighter, Dawes the Fireman and myself reached the top. As we reached the top, I went around to the side of the capsule where the man on the headset was hollering that the men were still inside the capsule. I was not sure who was inside, and I asked him specifically who was inside the capsule. He said that the astronauts were still inside. There were about five or six technicians standing on the gangway; and as I looked into the hatch, there were two men coming out that had been working on the hatch. Me and one other fireman, I'm not sure who he was - it, I believe, was Rector, we proceeded in without a mask and tried to take the hatch cover off. It was loose but was still intact. As we picked it up and down, we couldn't move it. We jammed it back and forth quite a few times, but the smoke was thick and we did not know how to take it off."

Burch's reference itself would confuse many by giving some the impression that the hatch was still on when the firemen arrived. However, a careful reading of his remarks shows that the hatch was open and Babbitt and Cuartolo were emerging when he arrived. Thus, he was not trying to open the hatch but remove it. Many other questions would also be asked about why there were not items in place when they were needed, as well as why the "fast elevator" was not in service that day. While corrections would be made, they obviously came too late for the three men trapped inside the module.

Meanwhile, those around them could only do the best they could under the circumstances. Burch continued, "I would say we stayed in around thirty seconds before we had to leave to get a mask because the smoke was too thick. Upon going out on the gangway, one of the men out there gave me a mask - gas mask - I put it on and entered the room again with one of the technicians. We then tried again to take the hatch cover completely off. He was trying to tell me that you had to drop it down and push it in and turn it sideways to get it off. We worked quite a few minutes on trying to do that. It seemed like minutes...I'm not sure how long it was. But, anyway, we could not get it; and we were choking up considerably on the smoke and fumes that were in there. We then went back outside, got a breath of air and then returning back, we tried again to get the hatch cover off. I know I choked up two or three more times, and the man that was with me also choked up. It wasn't but just a few seconds that he choked up so bad that he turned around and left."

In spite of the physical suffering they personally experienced that day, nothing was as frustrating as the problems they had trying to gain entry into the module, and nothing as disturbing as what they found once they made it inside. Burch remembered, "Frantically, I was still working on the hatch cover. I was shaking it, turning it, doing everything in the world I could to get it off. Then, just all at once it seemed to fall back on me; and as I turned with the hatch in my hand halfway off - someone was there to grab hold of one of the handles; and we set it back away from the hatch. Then, I took a flashlight, I laid over inside the capsule trying to see the bodies or anything that I could see. The inside was burnt considerably, there were wires hanging down. I shined the light completely around inside the capsule, and I couldn't see anything except burnt wires hanging down. I then backed out, told the man on the headset, I said, 'There's no one in there.' He said, 'There has to be someone in there. They are still in there. Get them out.'"

At this defining moment, Burch faced what was likely the worst moment of his career. "I re-entered, looked around again; and I still didn't see anyone but there under me was a boot. I grabbed the boot, pulled it, it came off. There wasn't anything there except just a black mask. Then, I just grabbed an armload of I don't know what; but it seemed like it was coming loose. The first thing I knew I had a pair of legs in my hand. The hair was still intact on the legs. They were not, burnt bad. In fact, they were not burnt at all it looked to me like. I checked to see if the skin was going to slip, it wasn't so I reached my arm through both legs, under both legs, and pulled up just as hard as I could pull. The body moved probably six inches or less, but I knew I couldn't move him out. I then backed off to see just exactly what I did have. I could see that the, just the knees were sticking up on the only person that I could recognize. As far as the rest of it, it was just a black mass and I couldn't tell which way the bodies were laying or anything. I then backed out. I told the man on the headset, 'They are all dead, the fire is extinguished. The only thing we need now is to get the smoke cleared out, and then we can tell more about it.'"

In concluding his remarks, Burch offered a final observation about his experience, and how he completed his search: "As I leaned in with the light, I crawled into the hatch and went as far as my knees, I looked around with the flashlight all the way to the back of the capsule; and I could not see anyone. At the time, the knees of the top man must have been under my stomach because I drew myself back and just grabbed a hand full of which just had to be a burnt suit and came up with a pair of knees. They had to be right at the hatch. As I leaned in, I must have been lying right on top of the knees. I could not see anyone in the back, but I could see full vision all the way to the back of the capsule."

While each witness would have his own opinion about how much time had passed at this point, audio recordings would later confirm that less than 10 minutes passed between the time of the first fire report and the moment that the final hatch was opened.

Chapter 7: Resuscitation Was Impossible

"Medical opinion, based upon autopsy reports, concluded that chances of resuscitation decreased rapidly once consciousness was lost (about 15 to 30 seconds after the first suit failed) and that resuscitation was impossible by 23:36 GMT. Cerebral hypoxia, due to cardiac arrest resulting from myocardial hypoxia, caused a loss of consciousness. Factors of temperature, pressure, and environmental concentrations of carbon monoxide, carbon dioxide, oxygen, and pulmonary irritants were changing rapidly. The combined effect of these environmental factors dramatically increased the lethal effect of any factor by itself. Because it was impossible to integrate the variables with the dynamic physiological and metabolic conditions they produced, a precise time when consciousness was lost and death supervened could not be conclusively determined." – Passage from the *Report of the Apollo 204 Review Board*

The doctors arrived a few minutes later, and while everyone who had seen the bodies had to figure it was too late, there might have been some hope among the medical professionals that something could still be done before they actually arrived. However, any hope was soon gone. According to the medical panel, "The two NASA physicians and the Pan American physician then proceeded to the spacecraft. The time of arrival at the White Room on the 8th level is estimated at 6:45 pm EST (23:45 GMT). When the physicians first arrived, the hatches had been removed, the spacecraft was still smoldering, pyrotechnics had not been safetied and smoke was too thick to spend any time in the vicinity without a breathing apparatus. After a quick evaluation, it was decided that nothing could be gained by attempting immediate egress and resuscitation. By this time, some 12 to 15 minutes had elapsed since the fire began. It was evident that the crew had not survived the heat, smoke, and thermal burns. Conditions within the spacecraft (later confirmed by toxicological determinations) were such as to produce high levels of carbon monoxide (CO), carbon dioxide (C02), and other toxic gases and irritants. Also, oxygen was markedly depleted after the rupture of the spacecraft. These conditions would have necessitated institution of resuscitative measures within a very few minutes, since under optimal conditions, resuscitation commenced more than four minutes after cardiac arrest is usually unrewarding."

Knowing there was nothing they could do, the doctors joined the growing crowd of those lingering around the disaster area. "The three physicians then returned to ground level until adequate ventilation could be established. Shortly thereafter, they returned to the spacecraft with equipment for an attempted removal. After trying to remove the Senior Pilot by cutting his suit umbilicals and electrical connections, it became apparent that extensive fusion of the suits to molten nylon from the spacecraft would make removal very difficult. For this reason, it was decided to discontinue efforts at removal in the interest of accident investigation and attempt to get photographs of the spacecraft and relative positions of the crewmen before evidence was disarranged. The two NASA physicians remained in the vicinity of the spacecraft while the Pan American physician returned to ground level. NASA Security arranged for photographic coverage. After this was accomplished, one of the NA SA physicians returned to the blockhouse for approval to resume egress operations. Approval was received from Major General Samuel C. Phillips, U.S. Air Force/Apollo Program Manager, shortly after midnight, local time, and egress was begun at approximately 12:30 am EST (05:30 GMT), January 28, 1967."

As mentioned above, the doctors performing their duties knew that there would be an extensive autopsy, and that the findings had the potential to prevent a future disaster. Therefore, though exhausted with grief and effort, they made sure the astronauts' bodies made it safely into the waiting ambulances for transport to their next destination. "The Pan American Dispensary log indicates that the ambulance with the Senior Pilot arrived at the Pan American Dispensary at 1:17 am EST (06:16 GMT). The ambulance with the Command Pilot arrived at 1:35 am EST (06:35 GMT) and the ambulance with the Pilot arrived at 2:08 am EST (07:08 GMT). Therefore, removal of the crew took approximately 90 minutes and was completed about seven and a half hours after the accident. The crewmen were removed to the Bioastronautics Operational Support Unit for postmortem examinations at 4:17 am EST (09:17 GMT)."

Few forms of death strike terror in the hearts of people like that of being burned alive. In the mid-1960s, when many homes still used fire as a source of heat for at least part of the year, these types of deaths were more common and thus more feared, so when word spread that the astronauts had perished in a blazing inferno, there were both gasps of horror and questions about how much they suffered and for how long. In fact, such questions continue to this very day among those who never accepted NASA's findings.

That said, the doctors were clear when they wrote that, in all three cases, "carbon monoxide poisoning is the most significant finding." The doctors went on to say that Grissom was the most severely burned, "estimated as 60% total body surface area (36% third degree)." White suffered burns "estimated as 48% total body surface area, (40% third degree)," and Chaffee was burned on "29% total body surface area (23% third degree)." While none of the men would have died immediately from the burns, the doctors admitted they were "considered as a contributory cause of death."

Despite the horrific extent of the burns, it still seems unlikely that any of the men suffered for long. In each case, the medical panel concluded, "Loss of consciousness was due to cerebral hypoxia due to cardiac arrest, due to myocardial hypoxia. Factors of temperature, pressure and environmental concentrations of carbon monoxide, carbon dioxide, oxygen and pulmonary irritants were changing at extremely rapid rates. ... The combined effect of these environmental factors dramatically increased the lethal effect of any factor by itself. It is estimated that consciousness was lost between 15 and 30 seconds after the first suit failed. Chances of re-suscitation decreased rapidly thereafter and were irrevocably lost within four minutes."

No one will ever know the sequence of events with certainty, but the medical panel did come up with something of a timeline indicating that, based on the biomedical readings, the astronauts became aware of the fire at around 6:31:04 and that at least one of the men was still conscious 42 seconds later. Beyond that, the panel also found that the "Command Pilot had moved from his normal position after the onset of fire. The suit failed prior to rupture of the pressure vessel (the time of spacecraft rupture has been estimated by Panel 5 to be 6:31:19 pm EST (23:31:19 GMT). ... The Senior Pilot did not leave his position until his restraining straps were burned through. He had moved from his normal position after the onset of fire. ... There is no evidence that the Pilot moved from his normal position after the start of the fire. This is consistent with the emergency egress procedure which calls for the Pilot to be the last to leave the spacecraft."

After extensive investigation, NASA concluded, "It was most likely that the fire began in the lower forward portion of the left equipment bay, to the left of the command pilot, and considerably below the level of his couch. ... The first stage, with its associated rapid temperature rise and increase in cabin pressure, terminated 15 seconds after the verbal report of fire. At this time, 23:31:19 GMT, the command module cabin ruptured. During this first stage, flames moved rapidly from the point of ignition, traveling along debris traps installed in the command module to prevent items from dropping into equipment areas during tests or flight. ... The fire was not intense until about 23:31:12 GMT. ... The original flames rose vertically and then spread out across the cabin ceiling. The debris traps provided not only combustible material and a path for the spread of the flames, but also firebrands of burning molten nylon. ... By 23:31:12 GMT, the fire had broken from its point of origin. A wall of flames extended along the left wall of the module, preventing the command pilot, occupying the left couch, from reaching the valve that would vent the command module to the outside atmosphere."

The second and third stages were worse, but also shorter. According to NASA's findings, "Rupture of the command module marked the beginning of the brief second stage of the fire. This stage was characterized by the period of greatest conflagration due to the forced convection that resulted from the outrush of gases through the rupture in the pressure vessel. The swirling flow scattered firebrands throughout the crew compartment, spreading fire. This stage of the fire ended at approximately 23:31:25 GMT. This third stage was characterized by rapid production of high concentrations of carbon monoxide. Following the loss of pressure in the command module and with fire now throughout the crew compartment, the remaining atmosphere quickly became deficient in oxygen so that it could not support continued combustion. Unlike the earlier stages where the flame was relatively smokeless, heavy smoke now formed and large amounts of soot were deposited on most spacecraft interior surfaces as they cooled. The third stage of the fire could not have lasted more than a few seconds because of the rapid depletion of oxygen. It was estimated that the command module atmosphere was lethal by 23:31:30 GMT, five seconds after the start of the third stage."

The doctors also weighed in on why the men died so quickly, including what problems within the module itself contributed to their deaths. They maintained "that the fire originated in the cabin rather than in the suit circuit." They also agreed that the fire "was most intense on the Command Pilot's side of the spacecraft," and the suits "were not capable of providing crew protection in a fire of this intensity." Finally, they noted, "Rescue personnel were inadequately equipped for a fire-type rescue."

Chapter 8: The Personal Tragedy

A picture of the Apollo 1 medallion, one of which was carried on Apollo 9

"By authority of the Administrator, National Aeronautics and Space Administration, the Apollo 204 Review Board was established January 27, 1967. This action was initiated through oral instructions issued by the Deputy Administrator, followed by written confirmation February 3, 1967, setting forth, in detail, the broad powers and responsibilities of the Board. The Review Board convened at Kennedy Space Center (KSC), Florida, on January 28, 1967, under the Chairmanship of Dr. Floyd L. Thompson, Director of the Langley Research Center. The sessions and organized activities of the Board continued at KSC until the Board submitted its Report. During this period an intensive review was carried out in accordance with the responsibilities placed on the Board by the Administrator. A principal element of this Review was the creation of 21 Task Panels manned by experts in their respective fields. The report of these Task Panels provided the main source of information from which the Board has formulated its findings and recommendations. Periodic interim reports were provided to the Administrator. With completion of this report, the Board has been recessed subject to being reconvened at the call of the Chairman." – Passage from the *Report of the Apollo 204 Review Board*

Naturally, Americans of all stripes wanted to know what happened with Apollo 1 and why. For one thing, sabotage was considered a real possibility by many; the Space Race with the Russians was a very heated affair, so it seemed perfectly plausible that they might do something to stop American progress. There were also allegations that NASA officials were incompetent, and that someone somewhere failed to do their job properly. Finally, there was the matter of financing, as NASA was coming under increased scrutiny to actually land a man on the moon. Many understandably wondered how the space agency could get an astronaut to the Moon and back if it couldn't even protect its astronauts on the ground here.

Of course, NASA not only had the responsibility to answer the questions but plenty of motive to do so in a satisfactory manner. Within minutes of the accident being reported, NASA sent in security personnel to secure Launch Complex 34, where the fire had taken place, but once the men were determined to be dead, there was no more hurry and investigators took their time in documenting the scene and everything in it. According to NASA's final report, "Small groups of NASA and North American Aviation management, Apollo 204 Review Board members, representatives, and consultants inspected the exterior of Spacecraft 012...A detailed inspection of the spacecraft interior was then performed, followed by the preparation and approval by the Board of a command module disassembly plan." Following this plan, the entire module was packed up and shipped to a hanger at the Kennedy Space Center on February 1. Over the next several weeks, it was dismantled, piece by piece, with every item and spacecraft components being carefully photographed and studied as it was being removed. As NASA later reported, "All interfaces such as electrical connectors, tubing joints, physical mounting of components, etc. were closely inspected and photographed immediately prior to, during, and after disassembly. Each item removed from the command module was appropriately tagged, sealed in clean plastic containers, and transported under the required security to bonded storage."

By March 27, 1967, the module had been completely disassembled and thousands of its pieces had been photographed and catalogued. Throughout the process, the priority remained the same: determine what caused the fire. According to the board's Final Report, "Throughout the disassembly operation, experts meticulously studied the exposed portions of the Command Module. The relative consumption of combustibles and sooting patterns were studied for clues as to the site of the ignition source. All structural elements, covers and panels were examined for evidence of association with the ignition. Component systems and parts were studied inch by inch with magnifying glasses and frequently parts were taken into the laboratory for microscopic or metallurgical analysis. Wire bundles were given particular attention and after separation, the individual wires were examined under 7-power magnification for sites of possible arcing. All components that showed evidence of abnormal fire effects were examined internally and many were tested for functionality. Many components showed burning of internal insulation or plotting material but in all cases they were exonerated on the basis of direction of flame travel or on the basis that there could be no communication with combustibles outside the component. Particularly suspect components were disassembled for detailed examination and analysis. All of the data developed by these visual and laboratory examinations were coordinated in making the final analysis as to probable ignition sources."

Meanwhile, another team was busy analyzing the data they had collected, beginning by creating a timeline based on "significant data that were obtained just prior to the report of the fire by the astronaut crew. These time lines cover the period of one minute before the fire report until all data signals were lost. The data shown includes signals from the gas chromatograph channel, the voltage of the AC Bus 2, the C-band beacon, the VHF telemetry carrier, the flow of oxygen into the suit loop, various indicators of spacecraft motion, the biomedical data from the Senior Pilot, and audio signals (voice and noise) received on the S-band communication link. An analysis of each item and a summary of their correlation follows."

After extensive and meticulous study, the Board asserted that "30 and 45 seconds prior to the report of fire, both the Command Pilot and Senior Pilot were active. The nature and level of the activity remain unknown. Except for the transients in data measurements that occurred approximately 9 seconds prior to the report of the fire, there are no other identified relevant events that preceded the fire. It should be noted that these data transients and subsequent activity of the crew may as easily be associated with the result of the fire as with the cause. The increase in oxygen flow to the suit loop prior to and immediately following the report of the fire and its effect on the pressure distribution within the suit loop is the result of normal demand regulator response to oxygen leaking from the circuit to the cabin. This is further compounded by the response of the regulator to the rise in cabin pressure."

The report went on to draw a number of conclusions, including that the fire was most likely caused by "an electrical arc in the sector between -Y and +Z spacecraft axes. The exact location... is [likely] near the floor in the lower forward section of the left-hand equipment bay where Environmental Control System (ECS) instrumentation power wiring leads into the area between the Environmental Control Unit (ECU) and the oxygen panel. No evidence was discovered that suggested sabotage." Furthermore, the investigators described the test conditions as "extremely hazardous" and admitted that the "rapid spread of fire caused an increase in pressure and temperature which resulted in rupture of the Command Module and creation of a toxic atmosphere. Death of the crew was from asphyxia due to inhalation of toxic gases due to fire. A contributory cause of death was thermal burns... unconsciousness occurred rapidly and that death followed soon thereafter."

Perhaps the most disturbing finding was that the men likely never had a chance of survival since they were "never capable of effecting emergency egress because of the pressurization before rupture and their loss of consciousness soon after rupture." To avoid a similar occurrence, the committee recommended "the time required for egress of the crew be reduced and the operations necessary for egress be simplified."

The committee also asserted, "Adequate safety precautions were neither established nor observed for this test." They based this conclusion on the following list of problems:

- "Those organizations responsible for the planning, conduct and safety of this test failed to identify it as being hazardous. Contingency preparations to permit escape or rescue of the crew from an internal Command Module fire were not made."
- "No procedures for this type of emergency had been established either for the crew or for the spacecraft pad work team."
- "The emergency equipment located in the White Room and on the spacecraft work levels was not designed for the smoke condition resulting from a fire of this nature."
- "Emergency fire, rescue and medical teams were not in attendance."
- "Both the spacecraft work levels and the umbilical tower access arm contain features such as steps, sliding doors and sharp turns in the egress paths which hinder emergency operations."

In response, the committee made a list of recommendations:

- "Management continually monitor the safety of all test operations and assure the adequacy of emergency procedures"
- "All emergency equipment (breathing apparatus, protective clothing, deluge systems, access arm, etc.) be reviewed for adequacy"
- "Personnel training and practice for emergency procedures [should] be given on a regular basis and reviewed prior to the conduct of a hazardous operation and that service structures and umbilical towers [should] be modified to facilitate emergency operations."

The committee also found the communication system "unsatisfactory" and suggested it be improved. They further called for studies to be done to see if the atmosphere within the module could be reduced from pure oxygen to some breathable mixture that was less flammable.

In all, the Review Board found a number of what they termed "deficiencies" in the "Command Module['s] design, workmanship and quality control." These included the following:

- "Components of the Environmental Control System installed in Command Module 012 had a history of many removals and of technical difficulties including regulator failures, line failures and Environmental Control Unit failures. The design and installation features of the Environmental Control Unit make removal or repair difficult."

- "Coolant leakage at solder joints has been a chronic problem."
- "The coolant is both corrosive and combustible."
- "Deficiencies in design, manufacture, installation, rework and quality control existed in the electrical wiring."
- "No vibration test was made of a complete flight-configured spacecraft."
- "Spacecraft design and operating procedures currently require the disconnecting of electrical connections while powered."
- "No design features for fire protection were incorporated."

In response to these and other findings, the Review Board made the following suggestions:

- "An in-depth review of all elements, components and assemblies of the Environmental Control System be conducted to assure its functional and structural integrity and to minimize its contribution to fire risk."
- "Present design of soldered joints in plumbing be modified to increase integrity or the joints be replaced with a more structurally reliable configuration."
- "Deleterious effects of coolant leakage and spillage be eliminated."
- "Review of specifications be conducted, 3-dimensional jigs be used in manufacture of wire bundles and rigid inspection at all stages of wiring design, manufacture and installation be enforced."
- "Vibration tests be conducted of a flight-configured spacecraft."
- "The necessity for electrical connections or disconnections with power on within the crew compartment be eliminated."
- "Investigation be made of the most effective means of controlling and extinguishing a spacecraft fire. Auxiliary breathing oxygen and crew protection from smoke and toxic fumes be provided."

All of the analyses made clear that NASA needed to fix the command module, not only because of potential problems on the ground but also ones that might take place in space. As the report pointed out, "Once the Command Module has left the earth's environment the occupants are totally dependent upon it for their safety. It follows that protection from fire as a hazard involves much more than a quick egress. The latter has merit only during test periods on earth when the Command Module is being readied for its mission and not during the mission itself. The risk of fire must be faced; however, that risk is only one factor pertaining to the reliability of the Command Module that must receive adequate consideration. Design features and operating procedures that are intended to reduce the fire risk must not introduce other serious risks to mission success and safety."

Chapter 9: To Pursue the Exploration of Space

"The Nation's space program requires that man and machine achieve the highest capability to pursue the exploration of space. Three gallant men lost their lives in the line of duty during the development of that capability. The Apollo 204 Review Board was charged with the responsibility of reviewing the circumstances surrounding the accident, reporting its findings relating to the cause of the accident, and formulating recommendations so that inherent hazards are reduced to a minimum. Throughout its proceedings, the Board recognized the need for an impartial and totally objective review in order to arrive at its findings. The Board believes that this was accomplished. The Board is very concerned that its description of the defects in the Apollo Program that led to the condition existing at the time of the Apollo 204 accident will be interpreted as an indictment of the entire manned space flight program and a castigation of the many people associated with that program. Nothing is further from the Board's intent. The function of the Board has been to search for error in the largest and most complex research and development program ever undertaken. This report, rather than presenting a total picture of that program, is concerned with the deficiencies uncovered." – Passage from the *Report of the Apollo 204 Review Board*

Webb and other NASA officials testifying before Congress

In addition to NASA's internal investigations, the United States Senate also held hearings to determine what went wrong and what should be changed in the future. With typical political tact, the Senate committee reported, "The committee recommends that NASA continue to move the Apollo program forward to achieve its goal. ... The Apollo 204 accident, however, may well cause the date for an American landing on the moon to be accomplished early in the next decade outside the schedule set in 1961. That would be regrettable. When set in 1961, it was a goal set for achievement and it was technically feasible. While this goal had attracted a great deal of attention in terms of national prestige, as pacesetter for the program and as rallying point for the people on the program, its true significance is seldom mentioned. The target date was and still is essential to efficient management of the program. It is essential to the planning process and to maintain a vigorous and competent organization. Any program and particularly the largest and most complex research and development program ever undertaken by man—the Apollo program—must have scheduled goals. The schedule is an essential and significant management tool—without it the program would require more and more time and more and more money."

The men on the committee knew they had to walk a fine line regarding what they wrote because their findings would likely be read with more interest than those of the average Senate committee. They also had to strike a balance between respecting the lives lost and casting blame, especially on one of the nation's most popular programs. "Safety must be considered of paramount importance in the manned space flight program even at the expense of target dates. The earnest declaration that "safety is our prime consideration" must be transfused into watchfulness so that people do not again stumble into the pitfall of complacency. NASA's creation of a Flight Safety Office with broadened capabilities and better lines of communication is a step in that direction. The Congress, in the National Aeronautics and Space Administration's fiscal year 1968 authorization act, directed the Administrator to appoint an Aerospace Safety Advisory Panel to review NASA's operational plans and advise the Administrator with respect to the hazards of proposed or existing facilities, proposed operations, and on the adequacy of [proposed or existing safety standards. The committee urges NASA to continue its post-accident efforts to achieve a high degree of safety in all of its operations and we recommend that NASA utilize the above-mentioned organizations to achieve the primacy in safety desired."

Still, there was one more piece that had to be dealt with: the Senate's own right and responsibility to oversee any government institution. Therefore, the committee concluded its remarks with a fair but firm warning: "Finally, the committee urges that the National Aeronautics and Space Administration keep the appropriate congressional committees informed on significant problems arising in its programs. During the hearings it was found that late in 1965 NASA found serious problems with the contractor's management of the contracts for the Apollo command and service module spacecraft and S-II stage—the second stage of the Saturn V vehicle. Notwithstanding that in NASA's judgment the contractor later made significant progress in overcoming the problems, the committee believes it should have been informed of the situation. The committee does not object to the position of the Administrator of NASA, that all details of Government/contractor relationships should not be put in the public domain. However, that position in no way can be used as an argument for not brining this or other serious situations to the attention of the committee."

Eventually, NASA was able to use what it learned from the disaster to make effective changes to the designs of the Apollo spacecraft. As one report later admitted, "As a result of the investigation, major modifications in design, materials, and procedures were implemented. The two-piece hatch was replaced by a single quick-operating, outward opening crew hatch made of aluminum and fiberglass. The new hatch could be opened from inside in seven seconds and by a pad safety crew in 10 seconds. Ease of opening was enhanced by a gas-powered counterbalance mechanism. The second major modification was the change in the launch pad spacecraft cabin atmosphere for pre-launch testing from 100 percent oxygen to a mixture of 60 percent oxygen and 40 percent nitrogen to reduce support of any combustion. The crew suit loops still carried 100 percent oxygen. After launch, the 60/40 mix was gradually replaced with pure oxygen until cabin atmosphere reached 100 percent oxygen at 5 pounds per square inch. This 'enriched air' mix was selected after extensive flammability tests in various percentages of oxygen at varying pressures."

There were a number of other less dramatic but important changes made to the module, including "substituting stainless steel for aluminum in high-pressure oxygen tubing, armor plated water-glycol liquid line solder joints, protective covers over wiring bundles, stowage boxes built of aluminum, replacement of materials to minimize flammability, installation of fireproof storage containers for flammable materials, mechanical fasteners substituted for gripper cloth patches, flameproof coating on wire connections, replacement of plastic switches with metal ones, installation of an emergency oxygen system to isolate the crew from toxic fumes, and the inclusion of a portable fire extinguisher and fire-isolating panels in the cabin."

NASA also used what it learned from the Apollo 1 fire to make improvements to Launch Complex 34. Among those were "structural changes to the White Room for the new quick-opening spacecraft hatch, improved firefighting equipment, emergency egress routes, emergency access to the spacecraft, purging of all electrical equipment in the White Room with nitrogen, installation of a hand-held water hose and a large exhaust fan in the White Room to draw smoke and fumes out, fire-resistant paint, relocation of certain structural members to provide easier access to the spacecraft and faster egress, addition of a water spray system to cool the launch escape system (the solid propellants could be ignited by extreme heat), and the installation of additional water spray systems along the egress route from the spacecraft to ground level."

While these and other changes made the space program safer, no one would ever describe it as completely safe, any more than one might describe air travel or driving a car as completely safe.

It was only possible for those in charge to minimize the risks while maximizing the rewards, and of course, the rewards were ultimately great. On July 20, 1969, two and a half years after the Apollo 1 tragedy, NASA scored its greatest success to date when Neil Armstrong and Buzz Aldrin finally planted their boots on the Moon as members of Apollo 11. One of the items Armstrong carried that day was a diamond-studded pin intended to fly with Apollo 1 and subsequently given to the agency by the three astronauts' widows.

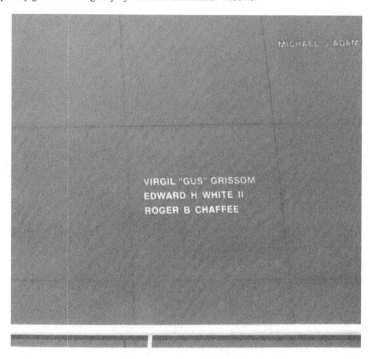

IN MEMORY
OF
THOSE WHO MADE THE ULTIMATE SACRIFICE
SO OTHERS COULD REACH FOR THE STARS

AD ASTRA PER ASPERA
(A ROUGH ROAD LEADS TO THE STARS)

GOD SPEED TO THE CREW
OF
APOLLO 1

Pictures of memorials to the Apollo 1 crew at Cape Canaveral

A modern picture of the launch pedestal used by Apollo 1

Space Shuttle Challenger

The *Challenger*

Chapter 1: Unusual Preamble to the Mission

The Space Shuttle *Challenger* was the second orbiter that NASA put into service during its Space Shuttle program. By October 1985 *Challenger* was one of four orbiters—joined by its predecessor *Columbia* and successors *Discovery* and *Atlantis*—that were in active rotation at NASA. Between *Challenger*'s maiden launch on April 4, 1983 and the conclusion of her ninth flight on November 6, 1985, she was the ship on which many of NASA's most celebrated achievements of the Shuttle era transpired.

***Columbia* Launching during STS-1**

On its second mission, STS-7, which launched on June 18, 1983, Dr. Sally Ride became the first American woman (and third woman in history) to fly in space. Ride's personal history would remain intertwined with *Challenger*'s long after STS-7 concluded on June 24.

The ship's third mission, STS-8, which launched August 30, 1983, made Dr. Guion "Guy" Bluford, Jr. the first African-American in space. In February 1984, on STS-41B, Bruce McCandless II became the first person to perform an untethered spacewalk. And the following October, on STS-41G, for the first time in history, two women—Sally Ride and Kathryn Sullivan—flew in space at the same time, with Sullivan also becoming the first woman to perform an untethered spacewalk.

Dr. Guion "Guy" Bluford, Jr.

After its seventh, eighth and ninth flights, which were Spacelab projects, *Challenger* was slated for a tenth mission, STS-51L, to take place in January 1986.

The planning phase for every manned spaceflight that NASA ever conducted began at least 12 to 18 months before the mission launched. During the Mercury, Gemini and Apollo programs, ships were designed as single-use vessels, thus requiring the long planning period. Back then, most of a spacecraft—as it existed when it launched—would be abandoned during spaceflight until the returning astronauts made an oceanic splash-landing in a small capsule upon their return to Earth.

Unlike previous spacecrafts, Shuttles were used repeatedly, enabling NASA to conduct missions more frequently than they had in the past. Crew selection and operational planning for Shuttle missions nevertheless took place at least a year before the flights were expected to occur. Coordinating all of the auxiliary technologies, such as satellites that would be deployed during flights, still necessitated prolonged planning periods even though, at any given time, the vessels were about four weeks away from being launch-ready.

Though spaceflight began to feel almost routine during the Shuttle era, shifting away from the special event atmosphere of the earlier NASA programs, the agency occasionally conducted missions that received more fanfare due to the technologies they were set to initiate or the presence of a noteworthy member of the crew.

By sheer chance, the history of STS-51L began earlier than those of most other flights, and it received greater public attention than virtually any other mission during the Shuttle program. The tragic fate of the mission directly altered NASA's future, resulting in flight cancellations and the suspensions of special programs. So it is impossible to know with certainty whether missions subsequent to a successful 51L would have garnered more attention. But if NASA's mission history played out the exact same way it really did, with the sole exception of a successful 51L, it likely would have remained the most publicly noted Space Shuttle mission ever flown.

The history of STS-51L and the reason for its popular appeal began nearly three years before its January 1986 launch.

During the mid-century "Space Race" many people envisioned a future in which space travel would be a common undertaking for ordinary citizens—in which the average American family would debate whether they should go to the Grand Canyon or the Moon for their summer vacation. Just as riding in an airplane was once a daring endeavor, travel by rocket could be refined and made safer over time. That collective aspiration to someday take part in dreams NASA brought to life played was integral to inspiring public interest in the space program.

But in the years following the 1969 Moon Landing popular enthusiasm for space travel waned. Dreams of vacationing like the Jetsons gave way to more grounded goals. And the level of interest NASA enjoyed never again compared to the culturally defining moments of the agency's most celebrated missions during the Mercury, Gemini and Apollo programs. The Shuttle program was further hindered in the public spirit by the fact that it had less illustrious goals than previous programs, and it lacked the competitive atmosphere that had enlivened missions during the Space Race.

By the mid-1980s, the United States was also emerging from a period of economic strife marked by recurrent recessions and high unemployment. The public misconception that NASA receives a substantial fraction of the nation's annual budget often compels many Americans to have a negative—or at least unenthusiastic—opinion of the space agency, particularly during difficult economic periods. (Even in 1967—the year in which NASA drew the most federal funding it ever claimed—the agency only commanded about five percent of the nation's total budget.)

NASA wanted to regain the relevance and popularity they felt they had lost. Their fixation on public support wasn't entirely motivated by vanity. If the public withdraws support from NASA, Congress will ultimately withdraw federal funding or shutter the agency altogether.

So, in 1983, prior to developing the mission specific to 51L, NASA undertook a new initiative that was not yet attached to any particular Shuttle mission. The "Space Flight Participant" program would send select civilians on the Space Shuttle, which NASA hoped would ignite public interest and broaden their ability to affect the lives of ordinary citizens. The program was chiefly a way of communicating that we might soon achieve the popular dream shared a generation earlier, when countless Americans imagined that they might travel to space.

The agency briefly considered sending *Sesame Street*'s Big Bird—portrayed in costume and voice by a man named Caroll Spinney—aboard a Space Shuttle. Though discussions between NASA and Spinney did occur, they quickly scrapped the plan when they realized that the Big Bird costume would not fit through *Challenger*'s hatch.

Administrators subsequently intended for the first civilian astronaut to be a professional journalist, who they believed would be well-equipped to communicate the experience to the public at large. Over 1,700 journalists applied. The most notable applicant was iconic CBS anchor Walter Cronkite, who was a constant and enthusiastic presence in network coverage of the Mercury, Gemini and Apollo programs. Newly appointed NBC anchor Tom Brokaw and ABC's chief White House correspondent Sam Donaldson also entered the race. Journalist Tom Wolfe, who authored *The Right Stuff* about NASA's first astronauts, the Mercury Seven, likewise applied to the program.

But when President Ronald Reagan formally announced the new initiative on August 27, 1984, he promised that the first civilian astronaut would be a teacher. Reagan was running for re-election that year, and he was hoping to win favor with a teacher's union.

NASA postponed plans to send a journalist to space and appealed to U.S. educators to apply to the civilian program. The chosen teacher would take a year-long sabbatical from his or her classroom to train for and undertake the mission. During the flight, he or she would conduct basic classroom science experiments on the Shuttle and teach science lessons from space, which would be transmitted live to schools across the country. NASA would pay the annual salaries of the selected teacher and a backup selection.

More than 11,400 teachers applied. During the first round of selection, they were reviewed by their respective State Departments of Education or other territorial or agency offices. Each state or other office chose two semi-finalists from the applicants, generating a group of 114 candidates. NASA conducted the remainder of the selection process, reducing the pool to ten finalists, who were announced on July 1, 1985.

The chosen ten traveled to the Johnson Space Center in Houston for a week of medical examinations, interviews, informative briefings and preliminary training, during which time they were evaluated for their flight-worthiness and public appeal. NASA intended for the selected teacher to draw attention from the general public as well as function as an effective if not inspiring educator.

The initiative, by then known as the "Teacher in Space" program, was not initially attached to any specific mission. It was only through sheer chance that the projected launch date for STS-51L ultimately coincided with the expected readiness of the first teacher astronaut.

NASA began planning for 51L in 1984 with an tentative launch date set in July 1985. But repeated changes regarding the mission's payload forced them to delay the launch to November 1985 then to January 22, 1986. The primary mission objectives would be to deploy a Tracking and Data Relay Satellite (TRDS) and deploy the Shuttle-Pointed Tool for Astronomy (SPARTAN) to study Halley's Comet, which was going to be visible from Earth in February 1986.

In January 1985, while teachers across the country were applying to the civilian program, NASA announced a five-member crew assignment for 51L.

Francis R. "Dick" Scobee was named mission commander for what would be his second spaceflight. A Washington state native born on May 13, 1939, Scobee was a U.S. Air Force pilot with a bachelor's degree in aerospace engineering from the University of Arizona. He was a combat aviator in the Vietnam Conflict, during which he was awarded the Distinguished Flying Cross and the Air Medal among other recognitions. Following his service he became an Air Force test pilot—a familiar career course for eventual astronauts. During his career, he logged over 6,500 hours in flight in 45 different types of aircraft. Scobee joined the astronaut corps in NASA Group 8, their 1978 class, nicknamed the "Thirty-Five New Guys," which was best-known for being the first class to include women (Ride and Sullivan among them). Group 8 also included Scobee's future crewmates Ronald McNair, Ellison Onizuka and Judith Resnik. He piloted *Challenger* during his first mission, STS-41-C, in April 1984.

Dick Scobee

Michael J. "Mike" Smith was named mission pilot for what would be his first spaceflight. A North Carolina native born on April 30, 1945, Smith was a U.S. Navy pilot who graduated from the U.S. Naval Academy and U.S. Naval Postgraduate School. He completed a tour in Vietnam, during which he earned the Navy Distinguished Flying Cross, three Air Medals and other recognitions. He subsequently became a Navy test pilot, logging over 4,300 hours on 28 different types of aircraft. Smith joined the astronaut corps in NASA Group 9, their 1980 class, which included future NASA administrator Charles Bolden.

Michael Smith

Ellison Onizuka was named mission specialist (1) for what would be his second spaceflight. A Hawaii native born on June 24, 1946, Onizuka was an Eagle Scout and a U.S. Air Force test pilot who earned bachelor's and master's degrees in aerospace engineering from the University of Colorado at Boulder. He logged over 1,700 hours during his pre-NASA career. Onizuka joined the astronaut corps in 1978's Group 8 along with Scobee, McNair and Resnik. He also served as mission specialist (1) on STS-51-C aboard *Discovery*, for which his commander was Apollo astronaut Ken Mattingly. Onizuka was the first Asian-American in space as well as the first person of Japanese ancestry to fly in space.

Ellison Onizuka

Judith Resnik was named mission specialist (2) for what would be her second spaceflight. An Ohio native born on April 5, 1949, Resnik earned a bachelor's degree in electrical engineering from Carnegie Mellon followed by a doctorate in the same field from the University of Maryland. Before and during her doctoral education, Resnik worked as a design engineer for RCA, which involved contributions to some NASA-contracted projects. She subsequently worked as a biomedical engineer for the National Institutes of Health. Resnik was recruited to apply to the astronaut corps by actress Nichelle Nichols—Lieutenant Uhura on the original *Star Trek*—who became a NASA recruiter later in her professional life. Resnik entered NASA in 1978's Group 8 as one of the first six women to officially join the astronaut corps. She became the second American woman to fly in space on the maiden voyage of *Discovery*, which launched in August 1984. Resnik was also the first Jewish-American in space.

Judith Resnik

Ronald McNair was named mission specialist (3) for what would be his second spaceflight. A South Carolina native born October 21, 1950, McNair earned a bachelor's degree in engineering physics from North Carolina A & T University and a doctorate in physics from the Massachusetts Institute of Technology (MIT), where he earned national recognition for his work regarding laser physics. He subsequently worked as a staff physicist at the Hughes Research Lab. McNair joined the astronaut corps in 1978's Group 8 along with Scobee, Onizuka and Resnik. He also served as a mission specialist (3) aboard *Challenger* for STS-41-B—when McCandless made the first untethered spacewalk. McNair was the second Black American to fly in space. He was also a black belt in karate and a skilled saxophonist. He planned to record a saxophone solo that he co-wrote during STS-51L, which would make him the first musician to record an original composition in space.

Ronald McNair

The crew began formally preparing for the mission at launch minus 37 weeks. In mid-July a would-be sixth member of the crew when Vice President George H. W. Bush announced NASA's inaugural selection for the Teacher in Space program.

Sharon "Christa" (Corrigan) McAuliffe was named payload specialist (2) for what would be the first Teacher in Space mission. A Massachusetts native born on September 2, 1948, McAuliffe earned a bachelor's degree in education and history from Framingham State College. She taught history and civics while her husband, Steven, a graduate of the Virginia Military Institute, studied at Georgetown Law School. She subsequently completed a master's degree in education supervision and administration at Bowie State University. Her family later relocated to Concord, New Hampshire. She taught history and English before becoming a social studies teacher at Concord High School in 1983, which was the position she held at the time of her application to NASA. Her classes included American history, law and economics as well as a self-designed course entitled "The American Woman." McAuliffe was a nearly life-long champion of the U.S. space program. She once stated, "When I was young, [American] women did not fly in space." Indeed, it was just two years before McAuliffe's selection that Sally Ride made her historic journey. In her application to the civilian program, the New Hampshire history teacher wrote, "I watched the Space Age being born, and I would like to participate." Though a science teacher may have been a more obvious choice for NASA, the evaluators judged McAuliffe to have the most broad and balanced ranges of interests and personal qualities of all ten finalists. Perhaps her most winning attribute was, as NASA official Alan Ladwig described, her "infectious enthusiasm."

Christa McAuliffe

McAuliffe's backup was Idaho elementary school teacher, Barbara Morgan. Every NASA mission is also assigned a backup crew, who complete training identical to the training program of the prime crew. A member of the backup team only replaces a member of the prime crew if the latter becomes ill shortly before launch. (It's a rare occurrence, but it has happened a few times in NASA's history.)

The basic experiments McAuliffe prepared to conduct during the spaceflight concerned chromatography, hydroponics, magnetism and Newton's Law. She also readied two 15-minute lessons that she would conduct from the Shuttle, which would be broadcast to U.S. schools. The first lesson was primarily a tour of the orbiter and an introduction to its basic components. The second lesson covered the scientific and social values of space travel.

McAuliffe wasn't the only late addition to 51L's crew. During the Shuttle era NASA occasionally launched a non-astronaut who was somehow affiliated with the program, either an employee of a NASA contractor that built Shuttle components or a member of Congress who supported the program. Non-astronaut members of the crew—McAuliffe included—were deemed "payload specialists."

Gregory "Greg" Jarvis was named payload specialist (1) for what would be his first spaceflight. A Detroit native born on August 24, 1944, Jarvis earned a bachelor's degree in electrical engineering from the State University of New York at Buffalo and a master's degree in the same field from Northeastern University. He served as a pilot in the U.S. Air Force for four years, starting in 1969. Following his honorable discharge from the military, Jarvis began working for Hughes Aircraft, the air and space manufacturer founded by billionaire aviator Howard Hughes. He became a communication subsystem engineer for Hughes, working on NASA-contracted projects. He contributed to and managed projects constructing telecommunications satellites. Jarvis was selected from a pool of 600 Hughes Aircraft employees to take part in a mission, gathering information about the design of liquid-fueled rockets. Hughes paid $40,000 to send him on the spaceflight.

Gregory Jarvis

Jarvis wasn't added to the crew until October 1985, which was rather late in the preparatory stages for the mission. Details regarding the 51-L's payload and the daily operational schedule for the mission were not finalized until the crew was complete, which pushed back some of the training.

The crew had to train for the flight in the Shuttle Mission Simulator, a duplicate *Challenger* cockpit with full instrumentation. Full simulator training began at launch minus nine weeks. Their time was occupied with a grueling workload of repetitive procedural simulations, including launch and landing procedures, Upper Stage deployment, rendezvous in space and use of the Shuttle's external robotic arm.

The mission activity schedule was also set, outlining the crew's responsibilities for the entire mission.

Day One: After arriving in orbit, the crew would check the TDRS satellite to ensure it was ready for deployment. They would deploy the satellite and the Inertial Upper Stage, which would require a series of separation maneuvers.

Day Two: The Comet Halley Active Monitoring Program experiment would begin. A Teacher in Space segment would be taped. And the engines would be fired to properly position the orbiter for the SPARTAN launch. Fluid dynamics experiments would commence.

Day Three: The crew would program the SPARTAN satellite, deploy it with the robot arm the maneuver to position themselves for separation from it.

Day Four: Experiments would continue, and the live telecasts of two Teach in Space lessons would occur.

Day Five: The crew would rendezvous with SPARTAN and recapture it with the robot arm.

Day Six: Preparations for re-entry would take place, and there was time scheduled for a crew news conference if NASA elected to hold one.

Day Seven: Final preparations for re-entry would take place, then *Challenger* would land at Kennedy Space Center.

The crew of STS-51L trained over 40 hours a week as they prepared for the mission, working through each active portion of their seven-day flight-plan. Despite the shortened training period, the seven crew members had no trouble achieving proficiency in all of their respective roles. Each one of them was thoroughly tested and certified by NASA personnel as flight-ready.

If only the same had been true of *Challenger* herself.

Chapter 2: Holding Pattern

Delays continued to bedevil the mission right up until it lifted off. Many specialists at Mission Control and technicians working on the orbiters contributed to all of the Space Shuttle missions regardless of which orbiter was used. Furthermore, due to the quick turn-around time between missions and the agency's mounting budget constraints, orbiters "shared" some mechanical parts. A Shuttle could not be flight-ready until the appropriate pieces were transferred from a returning orbiter to the vessel that was soon to fly. *Challenger* needed to borrow parts from *Columbia* before 51-L could launch. Before the end of 1985, the January 22 launch was postponed until January 23 due to the operational backlog created by the delayed landing of *Columbia*'s STS-61-C. NASA later moved the launch date to January 25.

Every mission had a "launch window," which was a timeframe on launch day during which the flight had to begin. The window was determined by Earth's rotational position and weather conditions. Each flight launched from Kennedy Space Center (KSC) in Cape Canaveral, Florida and had a designated Transoceanic Abort Landing (TAL) site in Africa or Western Europe, where the Shuttle could land about 25 to 30 minutes after launching if it became necessary to abort the flight. Weather conditions and time of day had to be considered for KSC and the TAL when determining the launch window.

The first-choice abort landing site for 51-L was in Dakar, Senegal. But Dakar was vetoed when it became apparent that local weather conditions that January would inhibit visibility (dust from the Sahara was clouding the sky). The back-up TAL, in Spain, was not a viable option because *Challenger* was going to have an exceptionally heavy payload, which would have made it impossible to shift north to Spain in an abort scenario. Casablanca, Morocco was ultimately chosen as the abort site, however it was not certified for night landings. So, 51-L would *have* to launch in the morning so that *Challenger* could make a daytime landing in Morocco if an abort became necessary.

Additional climate concerns prompted administrators to move the launch to January 26. Then, on January 25, NASA reviewed the next day's meteorological conditions for KSC and Casablanca. They determined that the weather in Florida—which was atypically cold that winter—would be unfavorable throughout next day's launch window. Temperature was a paramount concern. The Shuttle was only approved to launch in an environment that was 31 degrees Fahrenheit or warmer. The mission was ultimately postponed once again in hopes of avoiding an incoming storm and cold front. The Cape was expected to reach around 55 °F on Monday January 27, which were much more favorable launch conditions than January 26 would offer.

Vice President George H. W. Bush, who announced McAuliffe's selection as the first "Teacher in Space," was scheduled to attend the launch. But the repeated delays eventually forced the White House to cancel his appearance.

The astronauts and their immediate families traveled to Cape Canaveral in the days leading up to the anticipated launch. After reaching the Cape, the crew held a brief press conference to introduce themselves to the members of the media who were on-hand to cover the historic mission. Around 800 members of the press were credentialed to cover STS-51-L, which was nearly twice the number of journalists who attended the previous launch.

All of the crew members had spouses who would be in attendance, except for Resnik, who was not married. In place of a spouse, she invited actor Tom Selleck, for whom she harbored a well-publicized crush. Selleck was forced to decline the invitation, citing scheduling conflicts. Most of the astronauts' living parents also travelled to Florida, and the crew members with children were likewise joined by their kids. Christa McAuliffe's oldest child, nine-year-old

Scott, was accompanied by eighteen of his third-grade classmates and some of their parents.

On Friday January 24, the family members who passed NASA physicals—to ensure they weren't carrying any communicable infections that would compromise the health of the crew—attended a private picnic on the beach with the astronauts. Throughout the weekend prior to the launch, media coverage of the mission intensified, with Barbara Morgan and McAuliffe's parents, husband and son all giving television interviews.

Though NASA had access to the best meteorological information and analysts to determine the weather conditions as the launch approached, even the most skilled prognosticators managed to get the forecasts completely wrong. The agency briefly planned to launch on Sunday January 26, but delayed the launch until Monday after incoming weather data led them to speculate that Sunday would be stormy, windy and cold. But Sunday ended up having near-ideal conditions for a launch, which annoyed the crew slightly. And Monday was looking to be much colder than originally expected: It was shaping up to be no warmer than 40 F, which was 15 degrees cooler than the forecast. The environmental conditions would be acceptable but short of ideal.

The crew dined as a group with their spouses on Sunday evening—the night before the expected launch—in a quarantined dining facility. At the end of the dinner, McNair presented the crew with a magnum of champagne with an etched illustration of *Challenger* on the glass. The astronauts took turns signing the bottle with an etching pen.

The seasoned members of the crew slept somewhat comfortably on Sunday night, but their civilian counterparts were too anxious to sleep. Wide awake and fraught with anticipation, McAuliffe called Jarvis and asked him to keep her company. The pair left the crew quarters and roamed the area briefly until they found two bicycles that had lights mounted on their handlebars. They took a midnight ride around the complex, cycling through the cool night on a covert, private mission that was part exploration, part therapy. NASA administrators regulate the astronauts pre-launch activities with meticulous oversight to prevent them from last-minute illness or injury that could compromise the mission. (The planning was so rigid and detailed that their wakeup time the next morning was set for an otherwise unusual time: 5:07 a.m.) The training guidelines didn't address such extreme "renegade" behavior on the eve of a launch. But if agency officials were aware of McAuliffe and Jarvis' innocent attempts to exorcise their excitement, they said nothing of it.

The next morning, the crew reconvened in the quarantined dining hall for the traditional pre-flight breakfast complete with a cake decorated in frosting likenesses of mission imagery. The five career astronauts looked comfortable at the breakfast table, even Smith, who was about to embark on his first spaceflight. But Jarvis and McAuliffe's expressions betrayed their unique positions. Jarvis beamed a mega-watt smile; his hair was graying and thinning, but his sheer exuberance gave him the visage of a ten-year-old boy who had just won the lottery and the grand prize was a seat on a rocketship. McAuliffe looked both elated and preoccupied, no doubt contemplating the magnitude of the personal mission she felt she was undertaking—representing all of America's teachers for what were likely to be the two most dramatic lessons ever delivered in the nation's classrooms.

After breakfast, the seven crew members put on their sky blue mission jumpsuits. Then they made the well-publicized walkout to the van that transports the crew to the launchpad. The walkout is the last time that journalists are able to film or photograph the astronauts; it is also the last time immediate family members see their spacefaring loved ones. The crew waved to the cameras and their families. Everyone looked excited; McAuliffe appeared especially elated if not giddy.

The crew arrived on the launchpad platform, from which they climbed through Challenger's hatch one at a time. A member of the launch crew donned a graduation mortarboard over his scrub cap in honor of McAuliffe's presence on the mission flight. Each astronaut climbed into the Shuttle in an order determined by the locations of their seats in the crew cabin. By 7:56 a.m. all seven members of the crew were strapped in to their seats awaiting the launch.

At 9:10 a.m. the countdown was halted when a control panel light indicated that the hatch door either was not shut or latched properly. The launch crew believed it was shut properly, despite the warning light. Warning lights occasionally lit due to problems with their own wiring rather than problems with the more significant Shuttle components to which they corresponded. But if the launch crew was wrong and NASA launched anyway, an unsecured hatch could fly open during liftoff, causing the cabin to depressurize so rapidly that it would kill the crew.

Mission Control asked McNair—who was in a seated position that afforded him the necessary view—to visually confirm that the hatch pins were in secured positions. He did, leading NASA to surmise that they were being held up by a faulty indicator light. But as soon as they solved that problem another one presented itself. The crew on the launchpad was unable to remove the hatch handle, which they had to accomplish before the Shuttle could liftoff. The thread on the bolt that secured the handle to the door turned out to be stripped. Technicians requested permission from Mission Control to drill off the head of the bolt, which was granted. But they had to wait 45 minutes for a battery-operated Black & Decker to reach the launchpad— the volume of combustible rocket fuel made it too risky to use an electric drill, which could throw off sparks.

The drama regarding drills wore on. The batteries in the drill were dead, so the technicians waited another 30 minutes for nine replacement batteries to reach the launchpad. Eight of the replacement batteries were also dead; the lone functional battery proved insufficiently charged. Mission Control finally waived their objection to using an electric drill, but the cord for the drill turned out to be too short to reach the hatch. Once that problem was solved, the hardness of the bolt head broke a drill bit. The launch crew finally resorted to using a hacksaw to cut through the bolt. But, by the time they removed the bolt and handle, wind conditions at KSC had changed for the worse. The seven astronauts sat in *Challenger* for almost five hours before the launch was scrubbed at 12:35 p.m. NASA would try again the following day: January 28.

Students across the country were disappointed that the launch never transpired after spending the first half of the day parked in front of classroom televisions that were set to receive footage from the Cape. Broadcast reporters and evening news anchors ridiculed the space agency for having yet another multimillion-dollar mission delayed due to a "comedy of errors." And NASA officials were exhausted by the minor setbacks that seemed to perpetually hinder their plans. Perhaps, had the public considered NASA's history on that specific day, they would have been kinder to the agency's fixations on seemingly minor details. Had administrators thought more about the significance of January 27, perhaps they would have ignored the pressures that were about to cripple the agency for a second time in its history.

In NASA's then-28-year-history they had never lost astronauts in spaceflight. But they had lost astronauts. From 1964 to 1967, five astronauts were killed in training jet crashes before they ever flew in space. But, the agency's most devastating loss occurred on January 27, 1967 when the three-member Apollo 1 prime crew was killed while they conducted a training exercise on the launchpad. A fire swept through the cockpit during a routine launch simulation. Within seconds, the flames began burning through the astronauts' spacesuits, exposing them to an excessive volume of carbon monoxide generated by the inferno. The astronauts' official causes of death were asphyxiation followed by cardiac arrest precipitated by inhaling the poisonous gas. The men subsequently suffered extensive third-degree burns postmortem.

The Apollo 1 crew was particularly notable even before their shocking deaths. The Command Pilot was Virgil "Gus" Grissom, one of the Mercury Seven. He was the second American astronaut in space and the first American astronaut to fly in space on two separate missions. Senior Pilot Edward "Ed" White II previously flew on Gemini IV, during which he became the first American to walk in space. Pilot Roger Chaffee was preparing for his first spaceflight.

At NASA, the aftermath of the Apollo 1 fire was politically, institutionally and personally devastating. After the official investigation concluded, NASA was required to testify in front of Congress, some members of which openly called for withdrawal of agency funding. Subsequent missions were delayed 20 months while ships were redesigned. While many astronauts and NASA staff members personally suffered due to the loss of the crew, more than one agency official experienced a complete nervous breakdown. One case was so severe that the affected party had to be taken to a hospital in a straightjacket.

Several design problems contributed to the Apollo 1 disaster. NASA had been guilty of ignoring many ostensibly minor endangerments in the vessel. For example, there was an unnecessary abundance of flammable materials in the crew cabin; the all-oxygen environment was likewise detrimental to crew safety (in the event of a fire). Perhaps the more significant contributing factors were institutional problems. NASA had documented concerns about their primary subcontractor, North American Aviation, over a year before the fire occurred but opted to maintain the relationship with North American and continue using their designs.   NASA administrators wanted to handle the aftermath internally and resented the congressional and public scrutiny. They were chastised for their secrecy and evasiveness during the investigations. Ultimately, the agency's survival was owed largely to the continued support of President Lyndon Johnson, who still wielded significant power in the U.S. Senate.

NASA as a whole subsequently dedicated themselves to safety in a way they never had prior to the disaster. Losing three astronauts to a lethal combination of minor factors, many of which had been avoidable, scarred the agency in a way that seemed permanent. In 1967, most Americans would have believed that the specter of Apollo 1 was going to loom over all future missions, forever serving as a reminder that safety and precaution were paramount.

But a generation later, on January 27, 1986, as STS-51-L was postponed yet again, the public merely ridiculed the space agency for struggling to launch its own spaceships on time. And for all the attention that administrators fixed on atmospheric conditions and control panel warning lights, there were so many other questionable but seemingly trivial aspects of the ship and launch that they quickly overlooked. The nineteenth anniversary of the Apollo 1 disaster was noted on January 27: Its losses were remembered, but its lessons were dismissed.

Chapter 3: Unusual Conditions

January 28 was accompanied by a new, albeit expected, element in the launch equation: ice. An ice inspection crew began making trips out to the launch pad to monitor overnight ice development on *Challenger* and the launch tower itself around 1:35 a.m. At roughly 3:00 a.m. the decision was made to continue preparing for launch despite the sub-freezing conditions. Among the other pre-flight hiccups, a fire detector in a liquid hydrogen tank became faulty, requiring repairs. Ground crews were able to fix the hardware, but it delayed fueling for approximately two and a half hours. The crew's wakeup call was subsequently delayed one hour, but all of the astronauts were already awake by the time they were called to begin their own pre-flight routines.

Ice on the *Challenger* Hours before Launch

At no time during breakfast or any other pre-flight stage were the potential consequences of such a cold-weather launch discussed with the crew. But, even without formal acknowledgement, the crew must have known they were in uncharted territory with regard to launch conditions. The temperature that morning was around 28 or 29 °F, which was well below the temperature recorded at the previous coldest launch: 53 °F.

The crew for STS-51-L were all secured in their seats aboard *Challenger* by 8:36 a.m. Despite the frigid conditions, January 28 was gloriously sunny, creating a picturesque scene for a Shuttle launch. As the final ice inspection was undertaken just after 11 a.m., each astronaut and member of the launch team gave their official "go" for launch. For nearly three hours, the crew had been strapped in their seats, rendering them almost motionless, as they waited for the final nod of approval then—at last!—the final countdown to launch began. (Note: The official launch time is abbreviated "T" for launch time.)

T-30 seconds ... NASA announces the 30-second-mark in the final countdown procedure.

T-25 ...   **Smith**:   "Remember the red button when you make a roll call."

T-23 ...   **Scobee**:   "I won't do that; thanks a lot."

T-15 ...   "Fifteen" [seconds remaining].

T-6.566 ... *NASA gives the command to ignite Space Shuttle Main Engine 3 (SSME-3).*

T-6.446 ... *NASA gives the command to ignite SSME-2.*

T-6.326 ... *NASA gives the command to ignite SSME-1.*

T-6 ...   **Scobee:**   "There they go guys."

              Resnik: "All right."

              Scobee: "Three at a hundred." (indicating all three engines had 100%
thrust)

T+0 (11:38.010 a.m. EST) ... *Ignition of the Solid Rocket Booster engines (SRBs).*

              Resnik: "Aaall riight."

T+1 ...   **Smith:**   "Here we go."

The force and heat of the engines simultaneously shook icicles free from the launch pad and
melted them. Then, the Shuttle lifted off the pad, up and away, aimed toward the heavens.

T+7 ... *NASA asked Challenger to adjust its throttle to limit the maximum dynamic pressure,
    which was a routine maneuver that was executed perfectly.*

T+15 ...   **Resnik:**   "(Expletive) hot."

T+16 ...   **Scobee:**   "Ooohh-kaaay."

T+19 ...   **Smith:**   "Looks like we've got a lotta wind here today." (51-L was indeed
                          facing more dramatic wind shears than any previous Shuttle flight.)

T+20 ...   **Scobee:**   "Yeah."

T+22 ...   **Scobee:**   "It's a little hard to see out my window here."

T+28 ...   **Smith:**   "There's 10,000 feet and Mach point five."

T+40 ...   "There's Mach one."

T+41 ...   **Scobee:**   "Going through 19,000" [feet].

T+43 ...   "OK, we're throttling down."

T+57 ...	**Scobee**:	"Throttling up."
T+58 ...	**Smith**:	"Throttle up."
T+59 ...	**Scobee**:	"Roger."
T+60 ...	**Smith**:	"Feel that mother go!"
		"Woooohoooo!"
T+62 ...	**Smith**:	"Thirty-five thousand [feet] going through [Mach] one point five."

NASA instructed Scobee and Smith to undertake a routine air-speed indicator check.

T+65 ...	**Scobee**:	"Reading four eighty-six on mine."
T+67 ...	**Smith**:	"That's what I've got, too."

T+68 ... *Mission Control gave the order, "Challenger, go at throttle up."*

T+70 ...	**Scobee**:	"Roger. Go at throttle up."

Then, at T+73 seconds, the ship rapidly broke apart without warning.

That precise moment would ultimately be the moment that NASA marked as the end of STS-51-L.

Chapter 4: "Obviously a Major Malfunction"

No alarms alerted the crew or Mission Control to any malfunctions. Mission Control became aware of the problem when radar readings showed *Challenger* suddenly veering from its flightpath. At roughly the same time, a bright flash was observed at the ship's nose. Then, a series of component failures resulted in hydrogen and oxygen tanks rupturing, mixing and igniting in a sudden burn (not an explosion), creating a fireball that engulfed the Shuttle. The event dramatically increased the ship's air load factor to 20 G's (20 times the force of gravity), which was four times its 5-G limit. The increased force began ripping *Challenger* apart. A portion of the ship veered to the right, while another section, including the crew cabin, continued upward, propelled by the inertia of the launch. The fuselage was torn open; the sudden influx of air over-pressurized it, causing it to tear apart from the inside out and disintegrate. An external tank released propellant, which subsequently burned so quickly that it appeared another explosion occurred. It is critical to note that the Shuttle itself did not explode. Some external ship components exploded, the force of which caused sections of *Challenger* to separate.

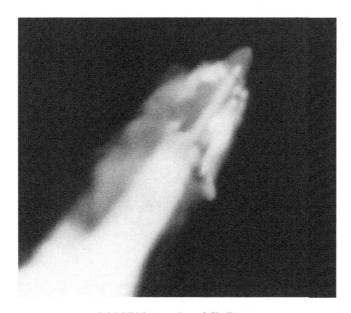

Initial Disintegration of *Challenger*

In the seconds immediately following the breakup, a voluminous cloud of smoke and water vapor lingered in the sky where the Shuttle had been when its flight suddenly came to an end around 48,000 feet.

Mission Control during the Breakup

When the breakup began around T+73, Mission Control lost radio contact with crew. Instead, flight staff heard several seconds of static as the ship tore apart. Even then, Mission Control was not really aware of what, exactly, had just transpired. At T+89 Flight Director Jay Greene instructed the Flight Dynamics Officer (FIDO, spoken like the dog name "Fido") to relay available information.

T+89 … **Greene**: "FIDO, trajectories…"

FIDO: (interrupting) "Go ahead."

Greene: "Trajectory, FIDO."

FIDO: "Flight, FIDO, filters got discreting sources. We're go."

Ground

Controller

(GC): "Flight, GC, we've had negative contact—loss of downlink."

Greene: "OK. All operators, watch your data carefully."

FIDO: "Flight, FIDO, 'til we get stuff back he's on his cue card for abort modes."

Greene: "Procedures, any help?"

Procedures:"Negative, Flight, no data."

They quickly began to understand what had happened and started initiating contingency protocols. At T+110—less than two minutes after the launch—NASA remote detonated the SRBs to neutralize the "free-flying" boosters so they wouldn't cause a secondary disaster.

NASA's public affairs officer Steve Nesbitt was providing broadcast commentary for the launch. He was following a script more than watching the liftoff, filling in specific flight data as it became available to him. Nesbitt was still delivering the pre-written dialogue when a flight controller began waving at him frantically, gesturing toward the sky. It took him several seconds to process the horror above. He waited several seconds longer before he began offering commentary again, delivering a memorable statement.

T+116 ...   **Nesbitt**:   "Flight controllers here are looking very carefully at the situation. Obviously a major malfunction."

Then, Nesbitt turned off his microphone.

One of the enduring myths of the event is that millions of Americans watched the launch and subsequent disaster in real time via live television broadcasts. In fact, few people were tuned in to the *Challenger* launch, though a greater-than-average number of schoolchildren were watching due to closed-circuit broadcasts to public schools so they could watch the start of Christa McAuliffe's mission. Only CNN was still broadcasting the launch live when the Shuttle broke up. The major networks only began to show the event after it began to unfold, playing taped footage of the calamitous event and its aftermath.

Many Americans became aware of the disaster, however, just minutes after it transpired. Millions of people watched (and re-watched) footage of *Challenger* shortly after it was lost, lending to the popular misconception that most Americans saw the event in real time. It is estimated that around 85 percent of the nation was aware of the story within one hour of the Shuttle's demise.

The tank explosions, quick burns of hydrogen, oxygen and fuel, and the ensuing fireball could easily give one the impression that the ship had actually exploded. But those events took place in such rapid succession that reality did not start settling in for the launch spectators and television viewers until the trail behind the Shuttle swelled, obscuring *Challenger*, then splintered. The site is rendered hauntingly tragic by the knowledge that those distant swells and splinters of smoke signal the moment, seemingly, when seven brave astronauts met their undeservedly violent fates.

Years after the fact, many people described the Shuttle disaster as one of the most memorable news events of their lives to that time. Specifically for people who were then too young to have lived through President John Kennedy's assassination, *Challenger* was *the* most significant collective event that they experienced until the O.J. Simpson's Ford Bronco chase in 1994 and the terrorist attacks of September 2001.

The loss of the Space Shuttle prompted a rash of questions from a public who—until that morning—had been largely complacent about the space program. During the Shuttle Era, flying in space became so routine to many people that they almost forgot what a dangerous enterprise it was. Few children had ever understood that space travel posed threats to the participants greater than riding in a car or airplane. Almost instantly, a national conversation was renewed about whether or not the space program was worth the financial cost and potential loss of human life.

President Ronald Reagan was scheduled to deliver the State of the Union address that evening. (Note: Claims that the White House prodded NASA to launch that morning against the agency's own wishes so that President Reagan could discuss the mission during his State of the Union speech were investigated by the Rogers Commission and discredited.) The President initially planned to deliver the State of the Union as expected but decided to delay the event after further consideration. Instead, he spoke to the nation from the Oval Office that evening to pay tribute to the *Challenger* crew and assert the nation's continued commitment to space exploration.

President Reagan's broadcast, written by speechwriter Peggy Noonan, went on to become one of the most memorable speeches of his presidency and one of the most significant speeches of the twentieth century, according to a survey of scholars in the late 1990s. In addition to reaffirming the country's commitment to space travel, Noonan sought to soothe the fears and concerns of America's children, so many of whom were either watching the launch live in their classrooms that morning or at least had a heightened awareness of the mission owed to the publicity surrounding McAuliffe.

As Noonan penned the address that afternoon, memories of a poem she often recited as a child, "High Flight" by John Gillespie Magee Jr., kept coming to mind. She included a quotation from the poem in her text, though she knew Reagan would only use the quotation if he knew the poem and, like Noonan, saw in it the same allusions to *Challenger*. It became the most iconic and identifiable passage in the speech.

"We will never forget them, nor the last time we saw them, this morning, as they prepared for their journey and waved goodbye and 'slipped the surly bonds of Earth' to 'touch the face of God.'"

After the broadcast concluded, Reagan and Noonan discussed the speech. The President asked her how she knew that he knew that poem so well. She replied that she hadn't known he was familiar with the text. The President told her that he used to read that poem every day when he took his daughter Patti to elementary school; the poem was on a plaque outside the school.

Three days later, NASA held a memorial service at the Johnson Space Center in Houston, though they were still weeks away from recovering the astronauts' remains. President and Mrs. Reagan attended the ceremony, where the President delivered a eulogy. Over 10,000 people joined the Reagans at the memorial, which *was* broadcast live by all the major television networks.

The Reagans at the *Challenger* Memorial Service

Numerous memorials followed in the months to come.

Chapter 5: Recovery

Following *Challenger*'s launch and loss, Jay Greene conducted an informal poll of the flight controllers to see if anyone received computer readings prior to the catastrophe that might have indicated malfunction. No one reported receiving any such data. They started trying to track the larger pieces of the Shuttle immediately after they realized what had taken place. At T+3 minutes, 25 seconds, the first pieces of debris were seen dropping into the Atlantic Ocean. Flight controllers maintained wide-eyed vigils at their monitors, analyzing the telemetry readings, attempting to discern where surviving pieces of the Shuttle might land and whether there was any possibility of recovering members of the crew alive. But, in the few seconds it took them to process the catastrophe, they also realized the answers to those questions: The debris would be scattered for miles in every direction and there was absolutely no chance any of the crew survived.

Little more than an hour after the launch, Mission Control had completely rededicated its focus to the search and recovery operations. Not only did they have to mount a search for surviving pieces of the ship, but they had to search their video and data for indications—any signs at all—

of what killed *Challenger*.

The agency's Range Safety Officer held recovery ships and search and rescue aircraft for an hour after *Challenger* broke-up, to give all of the debris a chance to land. The initial search was led by the U.S. Department of Defense and the Coast Guard, and it became the largest surface search in which the latter had ever participated. The search field covered 480 nautical miles and reached depths greater than 1,200 feet. That portion of the search process, which entailed recovering all debris from a restricted, code-named search field lasted for about a week. It became impossible to keep the search area secret and protected for long. And as the days passed, currents were scattering pieces of debris farther apart and sediment was starting to obscure the smaller pieces. On February 7, NASA shifted its efforts to merely recover debris that that could be helpful in the accident investigation. Salvage operations lasted until mid-April.

As soon as the search operations were under way, NASA embarked on what would prove to be a long-range effort to withhold information from the press and public. Some of the secrecy was warranted, such as their refusal to reveal the exact location of the search area—code named "Area 37"—to prevent people from scavenging the debris field for Shuttle fragments that they could stash or sell as macabre artifacts of the disaster. But other obfuscations were blatant attempts to mitigate the blame directed at them. In all practicality, the agency was simply unprepared to handle a catastrophe of that magnitude. Their conduct was ultimately dictated by the innate response people have when they feel they are under attack: they just wanted to defend themselves at all costs. As Rogers Commission member Robert Hotz later noted, "They were so smug about the idea that they would never have an accident that they had absolutely no plans or organization capable of handling it."

Despite a history of being open with the press even in the aftermath of great failure, NASA closed themselves off to members of the media and all other "outsiders." A general narrative of what had likely transpired was set and disseminated to the public. Journalists were afforded little opportunity to gain greater insight into the investigation. And the agency would not deviate from the set account unless they were forced to amend the story by new evidence that was impossible for them to obscure. Any attempt to compel more openness often yielded a terse declaration that NASA must be concerned only with their internal investigation. Outside questions would be addressed later at some interminable date. That statement was invariably followed by the shame-inducing reminder that seven astronauts had lost their lives, and it was incumbent upon everyone to avoid upsetting the families of *Challenger*'s crew by discussing the possible suffering the astronauts may have endured.

NASA's greatest misdeed, though, was in fostering convenient stories about the disaster then trying to suppress any information that betrayed a more damning narrative. The prime example of this offense was their account of the crew's fate. Since many people simply thought *Challenger* exploded, to most people it only seemed natural to conclude that the crew cabin likewise blew up, killing everyone aboard instantly. Given the circumstances, it was the version of events with which people were the most comfortable. If the crew cabin blew up with the rest of the Shuttle, then the astronauts could not have suffered physically. Instant death would also mean that they did not suffer psychologically in their final moments, aware of their impending deaths but unable to save themselves. NASA stated that version of events was accurate, save for the part about the entire ship exploding. They believed the only thing that would draw more public ire would be the revelation that the crew did not die instantly but suffered inexplicable anguish and fear for seconds or even minutes before they died.

But NASA officials knew before search operations even began that the more comforting narrative was—at best—possibly not true. They promoted that version nonetheless. As data and analysis demonstrated that the true course of events was almost certainly more grim, officials stuck to their original story anyway. When journalists asked about the possibility that the crew cabin did not disintegrate during the break up, NASA maintained that not only was the crew cabin lost instantly, they had film evidence to prove (which they never distributed, of course). All the while, a salvage vessel continued to venture out into the Atlantic Ocean day after day in search of vital debris, including a crew cabin that had not, in fact, disintegrated.

On March 7, divers from the recovery ship, the USS *Preserver*, entered the water to investigate "Target 67," a large chunk of debris found via sonar readings a month earlier. Target 67 could have been any number of missing pieces of the Shuttle. It was resting on the sea floor about 100 feet below the water's surface. Due to low visibility, it took the two divers a few minutes to get close enough to Target 67 to see it and identify what it might be. Around 90 feet, one of the divers could suddenly make out the legs of a white spacesuit sticking out of the debris, gently waving in the water. He was taken aback and returned to the surface as quickly as he could. Though the diver initially believed he had observed the remains of an astronaut, the suit was actually empty. The pant legs belonged to the type of spacesuit used during extravehicular activity (EVA) in space; it had been stowed in a compartment during the launch. But the suit's presence indicated that Target 67 might be the crew cabin, and that whatever remained of *Challenger*'s crew may have been found.

They returned to port for the night to report their suspected findings. A NASA guard quickly arrived threatening everyone from the *Preserver* about the consequences of leaking news of their discovery. Divers returned to Target 67 the next morning and were able to definitively identify the wreckage as the crew cabin after they found a piece of control equipment exclusive to that part of the Shuttle. At that point, their attentions turned to recovering the remains of the crew.

Being submerged for six weeks almost 100 feet down in warm ocean water affected the condition of the bodies in many ways. A lot of soft tissue (such as eyes and lips) was damaged by shrimp and crabs. Any remaining tissue had become colorless, delicate and gelatinous; in some cases, it became waxy, almost soap-like, due to hydrolysis. Some—perhaps all—of the bodies were not intact. Specific details of the autopsy results were never released, so it is publicly unknown if any of the bodies were fully intact.

Since the cabin wreckage was a hazardous environment due to the countless pieces of sharp metal protruding in every direction, the divers could only retrieve some of the remains without greatly increasing the risk to their own safety. The delicate nature of the flesh also necessitated that they undertake a very slow, gentle retrieval process. As bodies or body fragments were brought to the surface, they were placed in black plasticized body bag liners. Based on the position of the wreckage and the crew's seating placement during liftoff dictated the order in which the astronauts were recovered. Judith Resnik was the first crew member brought to the surface, followed by Christa McAuliffe. Divers working on the remains were increasingly concerned about continuing to retrieve the bodies from wreckage that could be compared to a nest of knives because it remained submerged in murky water, compounding the danger to the divers. Consequently, the decision was made to haul the cabin up to the ship deck to continue the process above water. They brought up a section of the middeck, from which a third crew member—likely Ronald McNair—was also recovered. Meanwhile, other divers located the crew cabin recorder, memory cores of the flight-deck computers and other flight-deck instruments.

Removing the crew cabin from the water did not prevent disaster from striking during the recovery process. As the team pulled another, heavier portion of the cabin out of the water, the motion and slight shifts in position that resulted from hauling the wreckage to the surface caused the remains of one of the crew members to dislodge from the cabin. The body bobbed to the surface, turned and sank just as quickly as it appeared, leaving the recovery team no time to retrieve it. It was the body of Greg Jarvis. Despite divers best attempts, they could not locate the body.

When the ship docked that night, another crisis erupted as NASA and the Brevard County medical examiner's office disputed who had jurisdiction over the remains and was therefore responsible for performing the autopsies. By law, the medical examiner had jurisdiction over that area of the ocean and was legally obligated to perform the autopsies. But the unique nature of the situation did cast some doubt over the matter, particularly since NASA was a federal agency. For their part, they wanted doctors from the Armed Forces Institute of Pathology to perform the autopsies, because employing military personnel would allow NASA to control the information that was released to the public.

Ultimately, NASA had control of the remains when they reached the shore, and they intended to retain possession of them. Since Kennedy Space Center (KSC) was not an area of exclusive jurisdiction, any potential accident at Kennedy would be handled by local police, which would result in the ME taking possession of the remains. To avoid this potential problem (as they perceived it), NASA officials opted to transport the crew remains to Patrick Air Force Base, which did have exclusive jurisdiction. The agency's legal counsel at Kennedy called the county medical examiner's office to inform them that their jurisdiction was nullified by presidential order. The chief assistant examiner, who was handling the phone call, protested, correctly arguing that a president didn't have the legal authority to simply overrule local jurisdictions. The NASA lawyer said he would send a copy of the presidential order to the medical examiner's office and also offered to allow the chief medical examiner to attend the autopsies. The ME's office never received a copy of the supposed presidential order; and the chief ME's invitation to view the autopsies was later rescinded.

On March 9, the *Preserver* returned to the water to continue the recovery process. At the same time, beat reporters at Kennedy were figuring out that a major discovery had been made during the recovery process. That evening, NASA caved in and formally announced that the crew cabin had been located and some remains were present. They claimed that out of respect for the astronauts' families they would not discuss the issue further.

The recovery process continued on the *Preserver*, ultimately yielding the remains of all the astronauts, with the exception of Jarvis, who remained missing. The team continued retrieving debris from Target 67 for more than a month, continuing to search for Jarvis the entire time. Though his body was spotted floating on the surface on March 9, it disappeared again as the team prepared to recapture it. Astronaut Robert Crippen, who NASA appointed to head the crew recovery process, became so anguished over losing one of the bodies that he personally paid for a scallop fishing boat to drag its nets across the seafloor in search of Jarvis' remains. But they found nothing. The *Preserver* concluded its recovery efforts on April 15. During that final day of diving Greg Jarvis was finally located, 0.7 nautical miles away from Target 67.

After several months of investigation, NASA ultimately pieced together a formal account of what transpired during *Challenger*'s final flight.

Examination of film from the launch and brief flight that followed revealed some critical insight into the Shuttle's failure. The first evidence of the cascading malfunctions came from footage immediately after ignition, when it was still on the launchpad. As early in the launch procedure as T+0.678 seconds, strong puffs of smoke were emitted from the right-hand SRB near the aft attach strut. It turned out that some technicians had observed those puffs of smoke but didn't say or do anything about the occurrence until after the disaster.

Gray Smoke Emitting from the SRB

On film, the clues became obvious when an unusual plume of smoke manifested next to the right aft attach strut at T+58.788. The plume had the same origin as the early puffs: hot gas leaking through a growing hole in an unsealed joint within the solid rocket booster.

The Recovered Right Solid Rocket Booster

The leak quickly gave way to a fire. At that point in the flight, pressure began dropping in an external fuel tank. Then, the right SRB pulled away from the attach strut. The force of the booster detaching from the ship caused a jolt, which the crew may have felt. Contents of the crew cabin recorder revealed that Pilot Michael Smith ominously uttered "Uh oh" at the same time the SRB began to detach. It was the last statement recorded. All of the equipment experienced total data loss from that point forward.

The crew cabin slammed into the ocean's surface at approximately 207 mph, which created a braking force 200 times greater than gravity. The force of the impact was greater than almost any other type of transportation-related impact that humans could endure. Portions of the cabin disintegrated. What remained of the compartment was instantly transformed into a three-dimensional jigsaw puzzle of twisted metal held together by an endless tangle of wires. The jumbled mass sank roughly 100 feet before settling on the seabed, entombing all seven crew members. The force of the blast in conjunction with the inertia of the Shuttle's liftoff had propelled the cabin to an elevation of 65,000 feet—roughly 17,000 feet higher than *Challenger* when it broke apart—before it began to fall in a torturously long descent. There were no protocol for, or even means for, a crew escape, such as an escape hatch or ejection seats. They remained strapped to their seats for the duration of the fall. The cabin was airborne for two minutes and 45 seconds after the flight was interrupted (at T+73).

The Crew Is Observed to Exit the Cloud

The astronauts had, in fact, survived the Shuttle's fracture. Evidence indicated that none of them even sustained serious injury from the force of the event. Their initial survival became irrefutable after wreckage analysis revealed that Michael Smith had flipped switches post-breakup; to adjust the switches in question, one had to pull them out and lock them, which tests conclusively established could not have been accomplished by a significant blast or impact. Also, four of the Personal Egress Air Packs (PEAPs) had been activated after *Challenger* broke apart, and that function could only be initiated by the deliberate actions of a crew member. Scobee and Smith's had to have been turned on by someone sitting behind them, likely Resnik. PEAPs for the other crew members were never recovered, so NASA was never able to ascertain whether all had been activated. The remaining air supply in the four recovered packs was consistent with the volume that would be present if the PEAPs were used for two minutes and 45 seconds—the duration of the cabin's free fall into the water.

Investigators were not able to determine how long any of the crew members remained conscious during the free fall. Rapid changes in altitude causes loss of consciousness without proper pressurization, which the crew may not have had because the PEAPs contained unpressurized air. If the cabin maintained proper pressurization during its descent, they may have been conscious until the end of the fall. In the very least, most if not all of the crew did know that a major malfunction had occurred. All of the evidence pointed to the likelihood that Scobee and Smith continued trying to pilot their ship until it impacted the water, while the other crew members engaged in every accident contingency they were trained to execute.

In late April, the remains of the astronauts were buried in accordance with their individual wishes. Dr. Judith Resnik, Dick Scobee and Capt. Michael Smith were buried (separately) in Arlington National Cemetery. Lt. Col. Ellison Onizuka was buried in the National Memorial Cemetery of the Pacific in Honolulu. Dr. Ronald McNair was buried in his hometown of Lake City, South Carolina. Christa McAuliffe was buried in the town in which she taught, Concord, New Hampshire. Gregory Jarvis was cremated, and his ashes were scattered in the Pacific Ocean. The recovered remains that were not identifiable were collectively buried in Arlington National Cemetery in what became the Space Shuttle *Challenger* Memorial.

Despite their constant assertion that utmost respect to the astronauts' families mandated not even *discussing* the possibility of crew survival, once the investigation demonstrated that the crew not only survived the Shuttle's break up but likely remained conscious long enough to know what was taking place, NASA wavered when deciding whether or not they would inform the *Challenger* families about those final hellish minutes. In the end, human decency won out. The families and subsequently the public were informed of, at least, the minimum to which the agency would publicly commit. NASA stated that while the crew survived the Shuttle's break up, they probably lost consciousness seconds after the crash, and their causes of death could not be determined. But even the three astronaut investigators personally acknowledged the evident truth: They were killed only when the cabin violently slammed into the Atlantic, and they were likely conscious, fighting their fates the whole way down.

NASA's internal investigation forced them to confront the reality of the *Challenger* disaster, but it would take an external investigation to ensure they accepted any meaningful measure of responsibility for the numerous avoidable missteps that led to the Shuttle's demise.

By presidential decree, the Rogers Commission would be convened to hold the agency accountable.

Chapter 6: The Rogers Commission

The Rogers Commission, which took its name from the chairperson at the head of the committee, was created by President Reagan on February 3, 1986 to formally investigate the causes of the *Challenger* disaster. The intention was for the Commission to operate independently from NASA but with the agency's full cooperation.

Members of the Rogers Commission Arriving at Kennedy Space Center

Sec. William P. Rogers was appointed chairman, leading to the committee adopting his name. Rogers served as U.S. Attorney General during the second term of President Dwight D. Eisenhower (1957 to 1961). He served as Secretary of State during President Richard M. Nixon's first term (1969 to 1973). At the time of his appointment to the commission, he was a partner in the New York City law firm Rogers & Wells.

Neil A. Armstrong was appointed vice chairman. The former astronaut was easily the most notable member of the panel, owing to his historic Apollo 11 Moon Landing in 1969. Armstrong was an astonishingly humble man (given his monumental role in human history) who never believed that he was due any more credit for the Moon Landing than any other member of NASA's staff, down to the secretaries and janitors. He still felt a deep connection to NASA and the manned spaceflight program, making the *Challenger* investigation, perhaps, a bit more personal for him than it was for most of the other committee members. From 1971 to 1980, Armstrong taught aeronautical engineering at the University of Cincinnati. At the time of his appointment, he was chairman of the board of Computing Technologies for Aviation, Inc. Armstrong previously served on the National Commission on Space, created to evaluate the nation's future in space exploration, which worked from 1984 to 1985.

David C. Acheson was a lawyer who previously worked as an attorney for the U.S. Atomic Energy Commission and as U.S. District Attorney for Washington, D.C. He had also been a vice president and general counsel for Communications Satellite Corp. At the time of his appointment, he was part of a private practice. Acheson was the son of Dean Acheson, Secretary of State to President Harry S. Truman.

Dr. Eugene E. Covert was an aeronautics expert who was teaching at MIT at the time of his appointment. Throughout the 1970s he was the Chief Scientist for the U.S. Air Force. He served as a NASA consultant on rocket engines. In 1973 he received the USAF Exceptional Civilian Service Award; in 1980 he received NASA's Public Service Award.

Robert B. Hotz was the editor of *Aviation Week and Space Technology*, an influential magazine, from 1955 to 1980. Among his many journalistic distinctions, Hotz received the Press Award from the National Space Club in 1965. In 1982, President Reagan appointed him to the General Advisory Committee of the Arms Control and Disarmament Agency—a position he held at the time of his commission appointment.

Maj. Gen. Donald J. Kutyna was a command pilot in the U. S. Air Force who also held a master of science degree in aeronautics from MIT. From 1982 to 1984, Kutyna served as the

deputy commander for space launch and control systems in the Space Division at Air Force Systems Command. In that capacity, he also acted as director of the Dept. of Defense Space Shuttle Program. In 1984, he became director of space systems and command, control and communications, Office of the Deputy Chief of Staff, Research, Development and Acquisition, at Air Force headquarters. His numerous decorations included the Defense Distinguished Service Medal, Air Force Distinguished Service Medal, Legion of Merit with oak leaf cluster, Air Medal with eight oak leaf clusters and Distinguished Flying Cross.

Dr. Sally K. Ride was known first and foremost for being the first American woman in space, which she achieved on STS-7 in June 1983, aboard *Challenger*. She was also the youngest American in space (a distinction she still holds), making her first flight at the age of 32. She returned to space in October 1984 on STS-41-G, also on *Challenger*. Ride was the only astronaut on the Rogers Commission other than Armstrong and the only person with flight experience in the Space Shuttle Program. Though she never flew in space with any members of the 51-L crew, Scobee, McNair, Onizuka and Resnik were all members of Ride's astronaut class, inducted in 1978, so she knew them rather well. Prior to joining NASA, she earned a doctorate in physics at Stanford. Ride was eight months into her training for a third spaceflight when she was appointed to the Rogers Commission, for which she headed the subcommittee on operations. She elected to forsake her would-be third spaceflight to join the panel.

Robert W. Rummel was an aerospace expert who served as a consultant to NASA, for which he had been awarded the NASA Distinguished Public Service Medal in 1979. He was the vice president of engineering of TWA from 1943 to 1959, a company for which he worked 35 years total. He was a personal aviation consultant to his TWA boss, Howard Hughes. He was elected to the National Academy of Engineering in 1973. Rummel was president of an eponymous company that consulted on aerospace engineering at the time of his appointment.

Dr. Arthur B. C. Walker Jr. was a professor of applied physics at Stanford University, a position he accepted in 1974. He specialized in solar physics, specifically the development of satellite telescopes used to record images of the Sun. He previously worked as a scientist for the U.S. Air Force and the Aerospace Corporation. During his professorship, his first graduate student was Sally Ride, with whom he served on the Rogers Commission.

Dr. Albert D. "Bud" Wheelon was a member of President Reagan's Foreign Intelligence Advisory Board as well as president of the space and communications group of Hughes Aircraft Co. Wheelon earned a doctorate in physics from MIT in 1952 before serving on the President's Science Advisory Council under Presidents Kennedy, Johnson and Nixon from 1961 to 1974. In 1963, he was appointed head of the CIA's Directorate of Science and Technology, where he pioneered the satellite technologies that became the nation's earliest aerial surveillance systems. He also work on surveillance and recon aircraft such as the U-2. The tools that he developed in that role were instrumental in directing the country's international relations and defense policies during the Cold War.

Brig. Gen. Charles E. Yeager was a retired member of the United States Air Force, in which he was an experimental test pilot. He rose to national prominence in 1947 when he became the first pilot to break the sound barrier. In 1953 he became the first pilot to fly at a speed more than 1,600 miles per hour. Yeager was an early favorite to be a member of NASA's first astronaut class (later known as the "Mercury Seven"). He was not interested in applying to the early program, however, because the first spaceships would have afforded him little opportunity to do any actual piloting. But, Yeager was Commandant of the U.S. Aerospace Research Pilot School (formerly the USAF Test Pilot School) from 1962 to 1966, during which time he trained many of America's Apollo Era astronauts, Fred Haise (Apollo 13), Ken Mattingly (Apollo 16), Charlie Duke (Apollo 16) and Shuttle Era astronauts Robert Crippen and Richard Truly, as well as fellow Rogers Commission member Donald Kutyna. Yeager was an aerospace consultant at the time of his appointment.

Joseph F. Sutter was a former engineer for Boeing. His leading role in the design of the Boeing 747, the jumbo jet that became a commonplace commercial airliner and cargo jet, has led to the description of Sutter as "the Father of the 747." A year prior to his commission appointment, Sutter received the U.S. Medal of Technology.

Dr. Richard P. Feynman was the most distinguished scientist appointed to the committee. (A 1999 poll in the academic journal *Physics World* had him ranked as the seventh greatest physicist of all time, behind only Einstein, Newton, Galileo and three others.) In fact, at the time of his commission appointment, he was one of the most well-known scientists in the world and arguably the most significant American scientist of his generation. Feynman was the co-recipient of the Nobel Prize in Physics in 1965. Though he was primarily a theoretical physicist whose most significant achievements were in the fields of quantum mechanics, quantum electrodynamics and particle physics, his personal and professional histories were peppered with technological, mathematical, artistic, literary, musical and governmental pursuits. Feynman was a participant in the Manhattan Project during WWII, which created the atomic bomb. He was present at the infamous Trinity nuclear test in 1945. Feynman subsequently received but turned down a job offer at Princeton, which would have allowed him to work alongside Einstein. After spending several years at Cornell, he accepted a position teaching at CalTech, where he would spend the rest of his academic career. Feynman was a great popularizer of physics who believed that the science should be made accessible to everyone. His use of humor in lectures and writing was extensive enough that he is often labeled a "humorist" as well. Feynman was mostly ambivalent about the space program at the time of his selection for the Rogers Commission. His scholarship concerned fields of physics separate from the fields related to space travel. He also held some less-than-glowing views on government bureaucracies following his time in the Manhattan Project. But, Feynman accepted the appointment because he felt an innate responsibility to use his uncommon abilities to answer the questions of how and why the disaster occurred. His willingness to participate in the inquiry was made even more dramatic because he was in the then seventh year of battling two exceptionally rare types of cancer (a fate not uncommon to members of the Manhattan Project, who were routinely exposed to radiation). By 1986, he knew that his time was limited. It was a testament to his fundamental drive to inquire that he was willing to spend what he knew might be the final months of his life laboring on behalf of a government program in which he had little to no personal interest. Feynman was initially at a disadvantage in some ways because he had no direct or indirect connections to any other members, who otherwise shared similar military, government or corporate aerospace experiences that could facilitate inter-committee partnerships.

It would be nearly impossible to overstate how valuable Dr. Feynman proved to be on the Rogers Commission. Though, not all of his fellow commission members necessarily valued his contributions.

The day after Feynman was officially added to the committee, he decided to go to the Jet Propulsion Laboratory (JPL), a NASA field office where some spacecrafts are built, to learn everything he could about the Shuttle. JPL is managed by CalTech, the university at which Feynman taught. So, he figuratively went down the hall at work for the briefing.

Feynman learned about the major parts of the orbiter, their construction and their potential failings. Among the most significant components were the Space Shuttle solid rocket booster engines (SRBs), which were the most powerful rocket propulsion devices ever flown. Each Shuttle had two SRBs, and they were responsible for the majority of the thrust during the first two minutes of flight. After the boosters burned out, the SRBs were jettisoned or released, then they parachuted into the Atlantic Ocean. NASA would recover the SRBs, inspect and refurbish them, then re-use them on a later mission. Each SRB began as seven individual steel sections, which were locked together with fasteners then sealed with two O-rings and heat-resistant zinc chromate putty. The O-rings and putty were supposed to ensure that propellant mixture and gases did not leak during use. But the JPL engineers also explained that hot gases had been able to penetrate the O-rings during some tests.

Had Chairman William Rogers been aware of the professor's self-initiated briefing, he surely would have been upset. Rogers was insistent about following procedure, ruffling as few feathers as possible and asking the minimum number of questions necessary to fulfill the basic role of the commission. To the group's good fortune, Donald Kutyna had experience on accident investigation panels and he explained how the commission *should* operate. But, Rogers insisted that, unlike Kutyna's past experiences, there was little information for them to gain about the *Challenger*, which was, of course wholly untrue. If investigators only asked the questions NASA was comfortable being asked, then, yes, there would be little knowledge to gain. But if they asked all of the questions that *needed* to be asked—particularly during hearings when NASA and subcontractor personnel were under oath—then they would establish a multitude of facts.

At the commission's second meeting (all of which took place in Washington), Rogers informed the members that they would begin their inquiry the following week with a trip to Kennedy Space Center. Feynman was "devastated" and "depressed" by the announcement. He was eager to begin the investigation immediately; he'd put the rest of his life on hold precisely for that cause! He implored Rogers to start right away. The chairman did not relent. Sally Ride told Feynman that she would be happy to work with him if he found something to do that would of use to the investigation. So he elected to travel to the Johnson Space Center in Houston (Mission Control) because he knew Ride would return to work at Johnson until it is was time for their scheduled trip to Kennedy. It took numerous conversations and outright begging before Rogers agreed to allow Feynman to travel to Houston. In the end, the chairman finally gave in, due entirely to the professor's persistence.

During a day-long briefing at Johnson, the physicist learned in greater detail how the Shuttle's engines, rockets and constituent parts operated. He also gained insight into NASA's strategy for addressing engineering weaknesses. If the reliability or safety of a Shuttle component was questionable, they largely ignored the need to address the weakness if it failed to cause problems on previous flights. The strategy was akin to reasoning that if a person has driven while drunk nine times without incident, it's reasonable to drive while drunk again.

Feynman got along reasonably well with most of the commission members, particularly Ride. Yeager only attended the first meeting for about 30 minutes before largely absenting himself from the rest of the proceedings, though he would later sign the final report. A few members proved almost as if they were attempting to thwart Feynman's fervent desire to actually answer the questions to the commission was created to answer. Rogers was certainly obstinate as was Alton Keel Jr., the executive director of the commission (who managed the many of its operational needs but was not actually a part of the committee itself). Surprisingly, despite Feynman's reticence of government officers, particularly military personnel, Kutyna proved to be the professor's greatest ally and the one with whom he struck up an actual friendship. Their relationship would ultimately be the key to Feynman's own inquiry and the success of the entire commission.

The day after his trip to Johnson, after Feynman returned to Washington, he received a call from Kutyna. Kutyna said, "I was working on my carburetor, and I was thinking. You're a professor—What is the effect of cold on the rubber seals?" Feynman immediately understood what his friend was saying. The fatal physical flaw that crippled *Challenger* was the O-rings diminished integrity in cold weather. The physicist immediately thought of the disparity between the launch temperature for 51-L (29 °F) compared to all of the previous Shuttle flights, the lowest of which had been 53 °F. What Feynman didn't know then, however, was that Kutyna's cunning clue was owed to a source who leaked NASA data to the major general that demonstrated NASA was aware of the O-rings' failure in earlier thermal tests. The source insisted on complete anonymity; their identity was known only to Kutyna. But the information they revealed would be the critical revelation that would make NASA's failures and culpability demonstrable to everyone.

Feynman attempted to get O-ring testing data from NASA but became ensnared in bureaucratic red tape. He subsequently requested an actual O-ring so that he could conduct his own tests, but NASA refused saying that each ring was custom-made for its expressed purpose and could not be spared. Then, it dawned on Feynman that the NASA office in Washington had an SRB joint on hand to use as a demonstration model, and it was complete with authentic O-rings. Feynman got permission to practice taking apart the joint in NASA's office. (They expected the joint to be used and even disassembled during the hearings.) Just hours before the commission was set to convene a televised public hearing, he went to a local hardware store to buy tools for the task, unsure of what he would need. Upon reaching NASA's Washington headquarters, he realized that the clamps he purchased were likely too large. So he went to borrow a clamp from the NASA medical office, a place he had come to know well. Throughout his tenure on the Rogers Commission, Feynman underwent testing conducted on behalf of his cardiologist, who was trying to help the professor manage his recurring cancer.

Feynman quickly dismantled the SRB with a pair of pliers then dunked an O-ring in a glass of ice water. He used the clamp to test the rubber's resilience under pressure when the material is cold. Sure enough, Feynman's hypothesis was confirmed: Once the O-ring reached a temperature around freezing, the rubber lost its resilience under pressure. At 29 °F the O-rings could not have been expected to seal the SRB joints properly. Shortly thereafter, the professor made his way to the hearing site, armed to make a demonstration.

Throughout the hearing, Feynman was restless with anticipation. But Kutyna—knowing his colleague's intentions—leaned over to him just as the hearing began and warned, "Copilot to pilot: Not now!" Feynman learned to trust his friend's advice after the first public hearing, when he cautioned "Co-pilot to pilot: Comb your hair."

Kutyna waited for the perfect moment in the discourse for the physicist to conduct his very public experiment. When he sensed the time was right, he prompted Feynman: "Now!" The professor's small show demonstrated many of the attributes for which he was already famous: keen curiosity, skill of inquiry and ability to explain an ostensibly complex science in a way that was accessible to everyone. The scene of Feynman dunking the O-ring in his glass of ice water became the most memorable image of the investigation, arguably of the entire post-*Challenger* ordeal. It grabbed the public's attention because it made the O-ring's failure so glaringly obvious. If its integrity could be compromised in a glass of ice water, what on Earth was NASA thinking when they tried to launch the Space Shuttle—the survival of which depended on the small pieces of rubber—in sub-freezing conditions?

More importantly, the revelation that the O-rings could only have failed at the launch temperature, elucidated the necessity in the weeks to come for a whole new line of questioning. Had NASA been aware of the potential for the O-ring's failure? And, how and why did they decide to launch STS-51-L that morning when it was so cold that it endangered the mission's safety?

The Rogers Commission finally made its long-awaited group field trip to Kennedy the day after Feynman's performance. At one of their briefings, the panel finally learned that while NASA's conduct communicated that the temperature was a minor concern at best that morning. But, as investigators would soon discover, it had not been of minor concern for Morton Thiokol, the subcontractor that built the SRBs.During a routine pre-flight conference call the night prior to launch, Thiokol engineers voiced concern that the rubber O-rings that sealed the joints in the SRBs had not been properly tested for launches that took place in environments below 53 °F. In fact, their "red line" launch temperature was 40 °F. Thiokol formally recommended that NASA delay the launch to a later, warmer date.

Members of NASA management, who were frustrated about the recurrent delays bedeviling 51-L, were emphatic in their opposition to yet another schedule adjustment. They argued that SRBs contained secondary O-rings anyway, which would seal the joints in the event any primary O-rings failed. Not surprisingly, subcontractors did not view themselves as equals to their NASA counterparts. And in the face of the agency's frozen resolve to launch on January 28 as long as cloud cover and wind speeds permitted (and even the wind proved questionable), Thiokol's manager backed off their assertion that the launch should be postponed. Similarly, officials at Rockwell International, which was the primary subcontractor for the Shuttles, were worried about the volume of ice on the launch tower on January 28. Rockwell feared that a piece of falling ice, rattled off the tower during liftoff, could knock loose a thermal protection tile. The concern was significant enough to them to warrant a launch delay. But when Rockwell engineers expressed the issue to NASA officials they—like Thiokol representatives before them—were not emphatic enough in their opposition to the scheduled launch. As a result, the launch sequence proceeded as planned with the exception of the delays prompted by the overnight repair to the hydrogen tank fire detector and ice inspections.

The committee spent two days at Kennedy, examining debris, photographs and film. When it was time for them to return to Washington, Feynman asked to stay. Rogers responded to the request, "I'd prefer that you didn't stay down here." Knowing what he was up against, though, he continued, "But, of course, you can do whatever you want." Feynman stayed, re-interviewing the people responsible for launch photographs and members of the ice crew.

Then, Rogers implemented a new strategy in his attempts to contain Feynman's zeal for fact-finding. He began to burden the professor with a cavalcade of requests—some for trivial pieces of information, some for meaningful data and some that were clearly attempts to drown Feynman in paperwork. It was apparent to Feynman what Rogers was attempting to do. What the chairman hadn't appreciated was that his counterpart was so sharp and rapacious when left alone to work that Feynman was almost always done with the meaningful and trivial fact-gathering tasks before he was even assigned them. And he had the good sense to just ignore the requests to find one sheet of paper amid the millions of pages NASA keeps archived.

Feynman's investigatory prowess finally started to impress Rogers, who began to see how letting the scientist operate as he wished actually aligned with the chairman's own desire to fulfill the commission's goals expeditiously. Furthermore, Feynman had exceptional success at recovering information for technicians, engineers and assembly personnel regarding the many disconnects in NASA culture. There were many instances when superior officers didn't talk to subordinates directly when it was warranted; there were countless memos from engineers to NASA management about construction issues that compromised safety and necessitated immediate action that they ultimately never received.

Though management insisted they had good communication with the engineers, Feynman quickly proved that they didn't. In a joint meeting with representatives of both factions, he asked everyone to write on a piece of paper what they believed was the probability of failure in a Shuttle flight. The engineers regularly responded each flight had a failure rate of one in 200, which Feynman determined was the accurate assessment when he analyzed the data himself. The manager present—after a lot of hemming and hawing, or "weaseling" as Feynman described it (to the manager's face)—eventually stated that the likelihood of failure was one in 100,000, which was inaccurate 500 times over.

Feynman, like all of the other commission members, wrote a report detailing all of the information he gathered. Then, the committee reconvened, for what the professor anticipated would be similar to a jury deliberation in which all of the members would debate and discuss the disasters causes and the improvements NASA could make to avoid the same mistakes. Instead, he was disheartened to spend the final meetings locked in fierce debates about "word smithing": Should we have a comma here? Lets re-phrase this sentence. How should we begin this paragraph? Then, there was the epic battle, which last for more than one day, about the color of and fonts used on the cover of the official report. Feynman thought it made sense to expedite the process by voting for the same cover color each time, but apparently several members repeatedly changed their votes. Eventually they chose red. It was published with a blue cover.

In spite of the fact that the committee concerned itself with such minor details as comma placement, Feynman was surprised to discover that the section he wrote, which he handed in to Alton Keel, was omitted entirely from the draft of the final collective report. In fact, though Keel promised to distribute it to all of the members, no one else had even seen it. It was a rather significant oversight for a group in which many of the members thought "red cover" or "blue cover" warranted days of debate. Feynman called Keel when he learned Ride had yet to read his report, insisting that she be given a copy. He had to call again when he discovered Acheson had not seen it either, continuing on until each member received one.

The committee was in favor of including Feynman's work, but there a dispute about whether it should be included in the main report or as an appendix (due to different writing styles). Feynman agreed to the appendix solution. After several instances of the office "losing" his report, he finally got it into the hands of an editor who tweaked wording (of course) but otherwise produced a polished version of Feynman's text. The editing and review process spanned nearly four months, and the commission began to draw to a close in June.

A final dispute erupted as the professor stood in the chairman's office the day after the commission's final meeting. The commission had agreed to a list of nine recommendations for improving Shuttle safety and NASA operations. Rogers casually mentioned that he wanted to include a tenth: an encouraging message that strongly recommended the president and nation continue supporting NASA. Feynman objected vehemently. It was absurd, contrary to their mission and not specifically asked of them in the president's directive. He likened it to the commission saying, "There's all these troubles, but in the end we recommend to keep on flying!" It was the same attitude NASA had that got it into trouble in the first place.

Eventually, he decided to present Rogers and Keel with an ultimatum: Drop the tenth recommendation and publish his appendix as it existed following its 23rd revision or he wanted his name removed from the report altogether. Rogers and Keel commissioned Kutyna to negotiate with Feynman. They stated that if the professor refused to accept the tenth recommendation, they'd retract their consent to include his report as an appendix. After protracted negotiations, Feynman agreed to cooperate if the tenth recommendation was not labeled a "recommendation" but only included as a closing thought. He also wanted the words "strongly recommended" changed to "urged" to diminish their weight. Keel tried hard to weasel around the constraints, calling Feynman one more time to ask if they could say "strongly urges." The professor replied, "No. Just urges." And so it was written and delivered to the president.

Chapter 7: NASA After the Rogers Commission

Following the *Challenger* investigation, NASA redesigned the SRBs for the remaining Shuttles—a process that was supervised by an independent commission. Space Shuttle *Endeavor* was built to replace *Challenger* in the orbiter fleet. The agency also created a new administrative department: the Office of Safety, Reliability and Quality Assurance. And in accordance with the safety protocols the Rogers Commission recommended, they adopted a less demanding launch schedule. It took 32 months of rebuilding and restructuring the agency, its Shuttles and its culture before the United States resumed manned spaceflight.

Many of the bureaucratic problems that led to the 1986 loss of *Challenger* were the same failings that contributed to the untimely end of *Apollo 1*. As the Rogers Commission wisely stated in their report, the *Challenger* disaster was "an accident rooted in history." In the immediate aftermath of each catastrophe, NASA reconfigured components of their spaceships and imposed institutional changes. But political and public pressures—with particular concern for agency funding, which is perpetually in jeopardy—ultimately compelled administrators, engineers, astronauts and subcontractors alike to settle back in to the endangering attitudes and practices that they previously held.

NASA's rededication to safety and pragmatism following *Apollo 1* eventually subdued, leading to the repetition of many of the same mistakes and, subsequently, the loss of *Challenger* and her crew nineteen years later. And, in a tragic repetition of history, the agency's renewed commitment to safety following *Challenger* likewise subdued, leading to the repetition of many of the same mistakes and, subsequently, the loss of Space Shuttle *Columbia* her crew seventeen years later on February 1, 2003. The seven-member crew of flight STS-107 were all lost when the Shuttle disintegrated during re-entry at the end of a fifteen-day mission.

The Columbia Accident Investigation Board (CAIB) was created to investigate the cause of the disaster. A piece of foam insulation broke off as *Columbia* lifted off, which was not atypical during Space Shuttle launches. But, in the case of STS-107, NASA believed more than an average volume of foam may have been dislodged. A piece of loose foam hit the leading edge of the left wing, causing a breach or opening in the wing. While the damage had little to no effect on the orbiter during its mission, hot atmospheric gases were able to seep into the wing when *Columbia* re-entered Earth's atmosphere. The hot gas caused the wing to break apart from the inside out, destabilizing the ship, leading to its disintegration over Texas, Arkansas and Louisiana. But the CAIB determined that the physical causes of the event were secondary to larger bureaucratic problems. Their final report stated, "the causes of the institutional failure responsible for *Challenger* have not been fixed."

Manned spaceflight operations at NASA were put on hold during the investigation, Shuttle modifications and organizational restructuring. Thirty months after the *Columbia* disaster, the launch of Space Shuttle *Discovery* on mission STS-114 marked the agency's return to spaceflight. But foam shedding during *Discovery*'s liftoff prompted another hold in the NASA's flight schedule (though the debris did not cause damage to the ship in that case). Engineers invested another year in making further adjustments to the orbiter fleet before missions resumed in 2006. Though the year-long pause to improve Shuttle safety demonstrated better safety practices on NASA's part, there would ultimately be no way to know if the improvements would have a long-lasting impact on the manned spaceflight program or if the changes would prove as fleeting as those imposed after *Challenger*.

Shortly after the *Columbia* disaster in early 2003, President George W. Bush cancelled the Space Shuttle Program. The final flight would take place when the joint endeavor to build the International Space Station (ISS) concluded (which was expected to transpire in 2010). NASA's Shuttle Era officially ended on July 21, 2011—one day after the forty-second anniversary of the Moon landing.

The agency never intended to fly Shuttles indefinitely. Low-Earth orbiters were always considered the next step in an ongoing progression toward grander and more distant missions. Many of the factors that doomed *Challenger*, however, ultimately imperiled NASA's ability to continue manned spaceflight at all. To say that institutional failures and flaws were the true culprit in *Challenger*'s demise would be accurate and fair. But the financial and political pressures imposed by Congress (which controls NASA's budget) and politicians who seek to use the space program as a device in their own political narratives were the true root causes for the agency's poor organizational structure and practices.

In January 2004, President Bush asked NASA to develop a plan for the successor to the Space Shuttle Program, with the primary goals of returning Americans to the Moon and reducing the costs of space travel. The directive typified NASA's eternal dilemma: the need to expand the boundaries of human exploration and knowledge but to do so as cheaply and quickly as possible.

When the United States first began working toward the Moon in the early 1960s, a lunar landing was essentially the agency's sole objective. So NASA was able to dedicate nearly all of its budget and manpower to achieving that goal. Each mission program was designed to gain the spaceflight experience and knowledge necessary to advance that goal. Project *Mercury* directly informed the missions of Project *Gemini*, which directly informed the missions of Project *Apollo*.

But, over the course of half a century, NASA became a different, much more diverse agency than it was when it cast its singular gaze on the Moon. It maintains numerous observational tools in space such as the Hubble Telescope and an assortment of satellites that monitor Earth's weather systems. Other NASA programs have launched planetary exploration vehicles and space probes to observe parts of our solar system to which humans cannot yet travel. And there are numerous other undertakings such as educational outreach to public schools and scientific research conducted onboard the ISS that also demand shares of agency resources.

Not only must NASA spread its time and budget across many varied programs, that budget has been perpetually shrinking since the final years of the Space Race. In 1966—which was the year that NASA received the largest portion of the federal budget it has ever been given—the space program accounted for less than four and a half percent of the nation's spending. In dollars and cents, NASA received approximately $0.0441 out of every tax dollar the federal government collected the previous year. By 1981, when the first Space Shuttle launched, NASA was working with a budget that amounted to about one-fifth of its all-time high ($0.0082 per tax dollar). Thirty years later, when the Space Shuttle was retired, the agency's share of the federal budget had dwindled to half of one percent, and it was still trending downward. (By comparison, 2011 defense-related expenditures—which did not include tax dollars spent on veterans' affairs— totaled seventeen percent of the nation's spending; Social Security was the most costly federal expenditure, commanding twenty-four percent of the budget.) In the 2010s, the agency's funding had diminished to the point that—to reduce spending—they began turning off fully functional satellites that still provided meaningful scientific data.

All the while, NASA has been perpetually threatened with even greater losses of funding. The constant threat of losing money when the agency is already underfunded forces administrators to pursue flight plans that are too ambitious and undertake projects that satisfy political goals before scientific objectives. Worst of all, it compels them to accept a level of risk well beyond the baseline risk inherent in rocket-powered space travel. To add insult to injury, NASA's program objectives have been manipulated by politicians outside the agency who seek to demonstrate their positions on certain issues.

The Columbia Accident Investigation Board specifically cited this confluence of financial and political pressures as a leading cause in both Shuttle disasters. The investigators asserted,

"Seventeen years separated the two accidents. NASA Administrators, Congresses, and political administrations changed. However, NASA's political and budgetary situation remained the same in principle as it had been since the inception of the Shuttle Program. NASA remained a politicized and vulnerable agency, dependent of key political players who accepted NASA's ambitious proposals and then imposed strict budget limits. Post-Challenger policy decisions made by the White House, Congress, and NASA leadership resulted in the agency reproducing many of the failings identified by the Rogers Commission."

Those same forces continued to converge on NASA as it attempted to establish its course for the post-Shuttle years. Within a year of President Bush's directive, NASA outlined and began preparing what was to be the next stage of manned spaceflight, the Constellation Program. Constellation was intended to overlap slightly with the end of the Shuttle Program to include the completion of the ISS. They also planned new boosters (rockets) and spacecraft for orbital and lunar missions.

President Barack Obama ordered a review of NASA and Constellation when he took office in 2009 to the best course for the nation to follow as it continued exploring space. The review was executed by a ten-member panel that included aviation officials, scientists, members of the military and former astronauts (among them, Sally Ride). They ultimately determined that Constellation could never be completed without a massive increase in funding, making it financially perilous to the space agency. They also advocated a more varied approach to space exploration, with consideration for travel to the Moon, Mars, Venus, asteroids and select planetary moons. As a result of their work, the Constellation Program was scrapped.

In 2011 NASA moved on to developing the Space Launch System (SLS), which is partly based on the Space Shuttle Program. The SLS is expected to carry out missions in LEO as well as travel to asteroids and the Moon. With further design evolution, it could be the system that carries the first astronauts to Mars.

But while NASA continues to look forward, the termination of Constellation was a significant blow to the space program. Their new course will require significant participation from privately owned space travel companies. While long-term visions for the future of space travel always allowed for the inclusion of corporate space-faring endeavors, many NASA supporters are critical of corporate-inclusive plans, arguing that space exploration has been and should remain the collective work of a nation. Five years after the final flight of Space Shuttle, the consequences of dwindling public enthusiasm for the space program grow evermore apparent.

Chapter 8: The Quarter-Century Riddle

On February 15, 1988, Richard Feynman succumbed to two forms of cancer, liposarcoma and Waldenström's lipoglobulinema, each of which is rare on its own to say nothing of their dual incidence. He was 69 years old; his death occurred almost two years to the day after his infamous ice water experiment during the Rogers Commission hearings. In those final two years of his life, Feynman's celebrity reached new heights, owing to that dramatic demonstration. His star only brightened in the years following his death, as succeeding popularizers of science drew attention to Feynman's works.

The great scientist detailed his experiences on the Rogers Commission in his second mainstream book *What Do You Care What Other People Think?* Among his recollections, Feynman described how, early in his *Challenger* investigation, he believed he was making significant discoveries and deductions all on his own but eventually came to realize that someone—a NASA or subcontractor source—was subtly guiding him to each revelatory piece of information in a bid to make known what they themselves could not reveal. The greatest example of this was General Kutyna's leading questions about starting a car when its parts were cold, which prompted Feynman to examine the thermal integrity of the O-rings. Though Feynman maintained a suspicion about who the guiding hand was, he died without ever receiving confirmation. That single unanswered question—seemingly the only question Feynman left unresolved—lingered in the years that followed *Challenger*, prompting ongoing speculation among amateur historians of the space program.

Feynman predeceased other members of the committee by quite a few years. Sec. William Rogers continued to work as a lawyer until the last months of his life. He passed away from congestive heart failure January 2, 2001. By then, he was the last surviving member of the Eisenhower Administration. Dr. Arthur Walker Jr. died in April that same year at the age of 64, following a battle with cancer. Robert Hotz died in 2006 of complications of Parkinson's disease. He was 91. And, Robert Rummel died in October 2009 at the age of 84.

Sally Ride ultimately never flew in space again. After the Rogers Commission, she was assigned to NASA headquarters in Washington, D.C., where she founded the agency's Office of Exploration. She left shortly thereafter to work at Stanford's Center for International Security and Arms Control. Ride was a leading spokesperson for NASA and various NASA public-outreach programs for the rest of her life. She also founded Sally Ride Science in 2001, which published books and other learning aids meant to entertain students—particularly girls—as well as inspire their scientific curiosity. She would go on to become the only member of the Rogers Commission who was also appointed to the *Columbia* Accident Investigation Board in 2003. Sally Ride died on July 23, 2012 less than a year and a half after she was diagnosed with pancreatic cancer. She was 61. Her death came as a shock to many because she had not publicly disclosed her illness. At that time, it was also publicly revealed that her passing marked the conclusion of a 27-year domestic partnership with Tam Elizabeth O'Shaughnessy, making her the first known LGBT astronaut. Sally Ride ultimately proved to be a woman of many secrets.

NASA was dealt a second blow only a month after Ride's death when Neil Armstrong passed away on August 25 at the age of 82, due to complications of coronary artery bypass surgery. Losing their two most iconic astronauts in the span of a month was particularly difficult for the astronauts corps, which its members and their spouses consider a family. Both Ride and Armstrong remained prominent advocates for NASA after their own careers in spaceflight came to an end. At one point, Armstrong even offered to return to space if it would compel political and public commitment to a program for manned missions to Mars. (Obviously, the nation did not take him up on the offer.) After the conclusion of the Rogers Commission, Armstrong joined the board of directors at Thiokol.

Albert Wheelon died in October 2013 at the age of 84. Eugene Covert died in January 2015 at the age of 88. David Acheson, Joseph Sutter and Chuck Yeager were all still alive, as of the thirtieth anniversary of the *Challenger* disaster.

So, too, was Donald Kutyna, who was promoted to the rank of General before he retired in 1992. And it would be Kutyna who, after a quarter century, finally solved the outstanding *Challenger* riddle. In 2012 he finally told the whole story about how he became aware of the O-ring's instability. Kutyna recounted that during the *Challenger* investigation a source slipped him a data sheet betraying NASA's secret: limited testing demonstrated that the O-ring's functioned poorly in temperatures below 53 °F. The source was so keen to protect their identity that the page they passed to Kutyna was plastic-covered, to prevent the passing of any traceable evidence, such as fingerprints, that could betray the source's identity if the page was ever discovered by NASA officials. The source wanted to pass the information to Kutyna because he was willing to be critical of NASA (unlike some on the commission) and he was the only member who had openly fostered a friendship with Dr. Feynman. Feynman was the one committee member who had no allegiance to NASA or a branch of the U.S. military or a government office. He was the only member who wouldn't be jeopardizing his entire career—his life's work—on revealing NASA's deception. And, so, the source passed the data sheet so Kutyna could lead Feynman to the pivotal discovery of the investigation. Without the disclosure and Feynman's subsequent revelation about the O-rings, the official conclusion about the disaster's cause may have remained NASA's official line that bad things just happen sometimes.

Back in 2012, Kutyna explained that he was only revealing the information because his source had just passed away, making it safe, after 26 years, to reveal their identity.

His source was none other than Sally Ride. In the end, it was the commission's lone Space Shuttle astronaut—the only one who knew *Challenger*'s final crew personally and whose own safety had been imperiled by NASA's willful negligence—who best honored the memory of the lost crew by covertly trying to compel their space program to better live up to its ideals.

Online Resources

Other books about the Space Race and Apollo program by Charles River Editors

Other books about Apollo 1 on Amazon

Other books about the *Challenger* on Amazon

Bibliography

Anderson, Clinton P. (1968), *Apollo 204 Accident: Report of the Committee on Aeronautical and Space Sciences, United States Senate, with Additional Views, Senate Report 956,* Washington, D.C.: U.S. Government Printing Office.

Benson, Charles D.; Faherty, William Barnaby (1978). *Moonport: A History of Apollo Launch Facilities and Operations.* NASA History Series. NASA.

Kranz, Eugene (2000). *Failure is Not an Option: Mission Control from Mercury to Apollo 13 and Beyond.*

Lattimer, Dick (1985). *All We Did Was Fly to the Moon.* Alachua, FL: Whispering Eagle Press.

Murray, Charles; Cox, Catherine Bly (1990). *Apollo: The Race to the Moon.* New York: Simon & Schuster.

Barbree, Jay/NBC News. "The *Challenger* saga: An American space tragedy." (2013)

http://www.nbcnews.com/id/3077897/ns/technology_and_science-space/t/challenger-saga-american-space-tragedy/#.Vos6C-l7ny9

Boyle, Alan/NBC News. "NASA Confirms Talks to Fly Big Bird on Doomed Shuttle *Challenger*." (2015)

http://www.nbcnews.com/science/weird-science/nasa-confirms-talks-fly-big-bird-doomed-Shuttle-challenger-n353521

Cronkite, Walter. *A Reporter's Life.* (1997)

Feynman, Richard. *What Do You Care What Other People Think?* (1988)

Gebhardt, Chris. "1983-1986: The Missions and History of Space Shuttle *Challenger*." (2011)

http://www.nasaspaceflight.com/2011/01/1983-1986-missions-history-space-Shuttle-challenger/

L.A. Times. "Robert B. Hotz, 91; Arms-Control Expert Ran Aerospace Publication." (2006)

http://articles.latimes.com/2006/feb/12/local/me-hotz12

Martin, Douglas/*New York Times.* "Albert D. Wheelon, Architect of Aerial Spying, Dies at 84." (2013)

http://www.nytimes.com/2013/10/03/us/albert-d-wheelon-architect-of-aerial-spying-dies-at-84.html?_r=1

NASA. "The Crew of the *Challenger* Shuttle Mission in 1986." (2004)

http://www.hq.nasa.gov/pao/History/Biographies/challenger.html

NASA. "Transcript of the *Challenger* Crew Comments from the Operational Recorder." (2003)

http://history.nasa.gov/transcript.html

Oberg, James/NBC News. "7 myths about the *Challenger* shuttle disaster." (2011)

Powell, Dennis E./*Miami Herald Sunday* magazine. "Obviously, a Major Malfunction." (1988)

http://www.lutins.org/nasa.html

Rogers Commission. *Report of the Presidential Commission on the Space Shuttle Challenger Accident.* (1986)

Sherr, Lynn. *Sally Ride: America's First Woman in Space.* (2015)

Sutter, Joseph. The National Academies Press. "Robert W. Rummel." (2009)

http://www.nap.edu/read/13338/chapter/51

White House via Ronald Reagan Presidential Library. "Appointment of 12 Members of the Presidential Commission on the Space Shuttle *Challenger* Accident, and Designation of the Chairman and Vice Chairman." (1986)

http://www.reagan.utexas.edu/archives/speeches/1986/20386c.htm

Made in the USA
Las Vegas, NV
08 April 2024

88415495R00059